Culinary Canvas

A Palette of Flavors

By

Alberta R. Kirkland

FRESHFRUITSANDCOMPOTE

Always select the best fruit, as it is the cheapest, and requires less sugar; and where every piece of fruit or every berry is perfect, there is no waste. Raspberries are apt to harbor worms and therefore the freshly picked berries are safest.

BLUEBERRIES

Wash and pick over carefully, drain off all the water, sprinkle powdered sugar over them and serve with cream or milk.

RASPBERRIES

Pick over carefully, set on ice, and serve in a dish unsugared. Strawberries may be served as above.

RASPBERRIES AND CURRANTS

These berries, mixed, make a very palatable dish. Set on ice until ready to serve. Then pile in a mound, strewing plenty of pulverized sugar among them. As you do this, garnish the base with white or black currants (blackberries look pretty also) in bunches. Eat with cream or wine.

STRAWBERRIES

Pick nice ripe berries, pile them in a fruit dish. Strew plenty of pulverized sugar over them and garnish with round slices or quarters of oranges, also well sugared.

BANANAS

May be sliced according to fancy, either round or lengthwise. Set on ice until required. Then add sugar, wine or orange juice. In serving, dish out with a tablespoon of whipped cream.

CHILLED BANANAS

Cut ice-cold bananas down lengthwise, and lay these halves on a plate with a quarter of a lemon and a generous teaspoon of powdered sugar. Eat with a fork or spoon after sprinkling with lemon juice and dipping in sugar.

GRAPE FRUIT

Cut in half, with a sharp knife, remove seeds, and sprinkle with sugar, or loosen pulp; cut out pithy white centre; wipe knife after each cutting, so that the bitter taste may be avoided. Pour in white wine or sherry and sprinkle with powdered sugar, and let stand several hours in ice-chest to ripen. Serve cold in the shell. Decorate with maraschino cherry.

ORANGES

Cut an orange in half crosswise. Place on an attractive dish, scoop out the juice and pulp with a spoon and sweeten if necessary.

PINEAPPLE

Peel the pineapple, dig out all the eyes, then cut from the core downward, or chop in a chopping-bowl, and set on ice until ready to serve. Then sugar the fruit well, and form into a mound in a dish. Garnish the base well with leaves or small fruit of any kind. You may squeeze the juice of one orange over all.

PEACHES

Peel fine, ripe freestone peaches. Cover plentifully with pulverized sugar, and serve with whipped cream. The cream should be ice cold. Peaches should not be sliced until just before dining, or they will be very apt to change color.

WATERMELONS

Use only those melons that are perfectly ripe. Do not select those that are very large in circumference; a rough melon with a bumpy surface is the best. Either cut in half or plug and fill with the following: Put on to boil some pale sherry or claret and boil down to quite a thick syrup with sugar. Pour this into either a plugged melon or over the half-cut melon, and lay on ice for a couple of hours before serving. If you use claret you may spice it while boiling with whole spices.

SNOWFLAKES

Grate a large cocoanut into a fruit dish, and mix it thoroughly and lightly with pulverised sugar. Serve with whipped or plain sweet cream.

TUTTI-FRUTTI

Slice oranges, bananas, pineapples and arrange in a glass-bowl; sprinkle with pulverized sugar, and serve either with wine or cream. You may use both.

RIPE TOMATOES

Select nice, large, well-shaped tomatoes, pare, slice and put on ice. When ready to serve sprinkle each layer thickly with pulverized sugar.

PINEAPPLE SOUFFLE

Take a nice ripe pineapple, grate it and sweeten to taste. Beat the whites of two eggs stiff and mix with the pineapple. Before serving, whip half a pint of cream and put on the pineapple.

FROSTED APPLES

Pare and core six large apples. Cover with one pint of water and three tablespoons of sugar; simmer until tender. Remove from the syrup and drain. Wash the parings and let simmer with a little water for one-half hour. Beat the white of one egg to a stiff froth and add one tablespoon of sugar. Coat the top of the apples lightly with the meringue and place in a cool oven to dry. Strain the juice from the parings, add two tablespoons of sugar, return to the fire and let boil for five minutes; add a few drops of lemon juice and a little nutmeg, cool and pour around the apples.

APPLE FLOAT

Peel six big apples and slice them. Put them in a saucepan with just enough water to cover them and cook until tender. Then put them through a colander and add the grated rind and juice of half a lemon, sweeten to taste and stir in a trace of nutmeg. Fold in the stiffly beaten whites of four eggs and put the dish on ice. Serve with whipped or plain cream.

APPLE DELIGHT

Put a layer of apple sauce in a buttered pudding dish, dot with butter, add a layer of chopped peaches and apricots, sprinkle with blanched almonds ground rather coarsely, repeat until the pan is full; pour the peach juice over the mixture and bake for one hour.

APPLE COMPOTE

Take six apples ("Greenings," "Baldwins" or "Bellflowers"), pare, quarter, core and lay them in cold water as soon as pared. Then take the parings and seeds, put in a dish with a cup of water and a cup of white wine, and boil for about fifteen minutes. Strain through a fine sieve, then put on to boil again, and add half a cup of white sugar and the peel of half a lemon. Put in the apples and let them stew for fifteen minutes longer. When the apples are tender, take up each piece carefully with a silver spoon and lay on a platter to cool. Let the syrup boil down to about half the quantity you had after removing the apples, and add to it the juice of half a lemon. Lay your apples in a fruit dish, pyramid shape, pour the syrup over them, serve.

BAKED APPLES

Take large, juicy apples, wash and core them well, fill each place that you have cored with brown sugar, cinnamon and raisins, and put a clove in each apple. Lay them in a deep dish, pour a teacup of water in the dish, and put a little sugar on top of each apple. When well done the apples will be broken. Then remove them carefully to the dish they are to be served in and pour the syrup over them. To be eaten cold. If you wish them extra nice, glaze them with the beaten white of an egg, half a cup of pulverized sugar and serve with whipped cream.

STEAMED SWEET APPLES

For this dish use sweet apples, and steam in a closely covered iron pot for three-quarters of an hour.

Quarter and core five apples without paring. Put into the pot and melt beef drippings; when hot, lay a layer of apples in, skin down, sprinkle with brown sugar, and when nearly done, turn and brown; place on a platter and sprinkle with sugar.

FRIED APPLES

Quarter and core five apples without paring. Put into a frying-pan one cup of sugar, one tablespoon of butter and three tablespoons of water. Let this melt and lay in the apples with the skin up. Cover and fry slowly until brown.

APPLE SAUCE VICTORIA

Pare, quarter and core the apples. Set on to boil in cold water, and boil them over a very brisk fire; when they are soft mash with a potato masher and pass the mashed apples through a sieve. Sweeten to taste and flavor with a teaspoon of vanilla. This way of seasoning apples is highly recommended, especially if they are tasteless.

PEACH COMPOTE

Pare the fruit, leave it whole and put on to boil with sweetened water. Add a few cloves (remove the heads), also a stick of cinnamon bark. Boil the peaches until tender, then take up with a perforated skimmer and lay them in your fruit dish. Boil the syrup until thick, then pour over the peaches. Eat cold with sweet cream. Common cheap peaches make a very nice dessert, cooked in the above manner, clings especially, which cannot be used to cut up.

COMPOTE OF RASPBERRIES

Make a syrup of half a pound of sugar and half a cup of water, put into it one quart of berries which have been carefully picked and washed. Boil up once. Serve cold.

COMPOTE OF PINEAPPLE

Cut off the rind of a pineapple, core and trim out all the eyes. Cut into desired slices. Set on to boil with half a pound of sugar, and the juice of one or two tart oranges. When the pineapple is tender and clear, put into a compote dish and boil the syrup until clear. Pour over all and cool. The addition of a wineglass of brandy improves this compote very much.

COMPOTE OF PEARS

It is not necessary to take a fine quality of pears for this purpose. Pare the fruit, leaving on the stems, and stew in sugar and a very little water. Flavor with stick cinnamon and a few cloves (take out the head of each clove) and when soft place each pear carefully on a platter until cold. Then arrange them nicely in a glass bowl or flat glass dish, the stems all on the outer rim. Pour over them the sauce, which should be boiled thick like syrup. Eat cold.

HUCKLEBERRY COMPOTE

Pick over a quart of huckleberries or blueberries, wash them and set to boil. Do not add any water to them. Sweeten with half a cup of sugar, and spice with half a teaspoon of cinnamon. Just before removing from the fire, add a teaspoon of cornstarch which has been wet with a little cold water. Do this thoroughly in a cup and stir with a teaspoon so as not to have any lumps in it. Pour into a glass bowl. Eat cold.

RHUBARB SAUCE

Strip the skin off the stalks with care, cut them into small pieces, put into a saucepan with very little water, and stew slowly until soft. Sweeten while hot, but do not boil the sugar with the fruit. Eat cold. Very wholesome.

BAKED RHUBARB

Peel and cut into two-inch lengths three bunches of rhubarb. Dredge with flour and put in baking dish with one cup of sugar sprinkled over. Bake in moderate oven three-quarters of an hour. Very nice served hot as a vegetable, or cold as a sauce.

FIG SAUCE

Stew figs slowly for two hours, until soft; sweeten with loaf sugar, about two tablespoons to a pound of fruit; add a glass of port or other wine and a little lemon juice. Serve when cold.

DRIED FRUITS

To cook dried fruits thoroughly they should after careful washing be soaked overnight. Next morning put them over the fire in the water in which they have been soaked; bring to a boil; then simmer slowly until the fruit is thoroughly cooked but not broken. Sweeten to taste. Very much less sugar will be needed than for fresh fruit.

STEWED PRUNES

Cleanse thoroughly, soak in water ten or twelve hours, adding a little granulated sugar when putting to soak, for although the fruit is sweet enough, yet experience has shown that the added sugar changes by chemical process into fruit sugar and brings out better the flavor of the fruit. After soaking, the fruit will assume its full size, and is ready to be simmered on the back of the stove. Do not boil prunes, that is what spoils them. Simmer, simmer only. Keep lid on. Shake gently, do not stir, and never let boil. When tender they are ready for table. Serve cold, and a little cream will make them more delicious. A little claret or sauterne poured over the prunes just as cooking is finished adds a flavor relished by many. Added just before simmering, a little sliced lemon or orange gives a rich color and flavor to the syrup.

BAKED PRUNES

Cook prunes in an earthenware bean pot in the oven. Wash and soak the prunes and put them in the pot with a very little water; let them cook slowly for a long time. They will be found delicious, thick and rich, without any of the objectionable sweetness. Lemon, juice and peel, may be added if desired.

PRUNES WITHOUT SUGAR

Wash prunes thoroughly, pour boiling water over same and let them stand for ten minutes. Then drain and pour boiling water over them again; put in sealed jar; see that prunes are all covered with water. Ready for use after forty-eight hours. Will keep for a week at a time and the longer they stand the thicker the syrup gets.

STEAMED PRUNES

Steam until the fruit is swollen to its original size and is tender. Sprinkle with powdered sugar and squeeze lemon juice over them.

PRUNE SOUFFLE

Remove the pits from a large cup of stewed prunes and chop fine. Add the whites of three eggs and a half cup of sugar beaten to a stiff froth. Mix well, turn into a buttered dish and bake thirty minutes in a moderate oven. Serve with whipped cream. If it is desired to cook this in individual cups, butter the cups, fill only two-thirds full, to allow for puffing up of the eggs, and set the cup a in a pan of water to bake. Some like a dash of cinnamon in this.

SWEET ENTREE OF RIPE PEACHES

Take large, solid peaches, pour boiling water over them so that the skin may be removed smoothly. Have ready thick syrup made of sugar and water. When boiling hot add peaches and boil about five minutes; remove and place in ice chest. When ready to serve have a sweet cracker on dish, place peach on same and pour over this a raspberry jelly slightly thinned and cover all with salted almonds or walnuts. Other fruits may be treated in like manner.

MEHLSPEISE (FLOUR FOODS)

NOODLES

Beat three whole eggs very light and sift in sufficient flour to make a stiff paste. Work until smooth, break off a piece and roll out on board very thin. Break oft another piece and roll and continue until all is used. Let rolled-out dough dry, then cut all except one piece in long strips one inch wide. Fold the one piece in layers and cut very fine noodles. Boil large noodles in pot of salted boiling water, drain in colander when tender and stir in two tablespoons of butter. Heat a tablespoon of butter in the frying-pan and brown fine noodles in this butter. Sprinkle these over the broad noodles, pour a cup of milk over the whole and brown in stove. Serve in same dish in which it was baked.

BROAD NOODLES

Make noodles as above and when drained sprinkle with fine noodles which have been browned in two tablespoons of sweet dripping; serve as a vegetable. If so desired, a cup of soup stock may be added and noodles browned in stove. Serve hot.

NOODLES WITH BUTTER

Plunge one pound of noodles into two quarts of boiling water and cook for fifteen minutes. Drain well, replace in the same pan, season with one-half teaspoon of salt, two teaspoons of white pepper, adding one ounce good butter. Gently mix without breaking the noodles until the butter is thoroughly dissolved, and serve.

NOODLES WITH CHEESE

If you make the noodles at home, use two eggs for the dough; if you buy macaroni use one-quarter of a pound, cut up and boil in salt water; boil about fifteen minutes; drain off the water and let cold water run through them; grate a cup of cheese; melt a piece of fresh butter, about the size of an egg, in a saucepan, stir in a heaping tablespoon of flour, add gradually to this a pint of rich milk, stirring constantly; take from the fire as it thickens. Butter a pudding dish, lay in a layer of noodles, then cheese, then sauce, then begin with noodles again until all is used up. Sprinkle cheese on top, a few cracker crumbs and flakes of butter here and there. Bake until brown.

NOODLES AND APPLES

Peel and cut six apples. Take broad noodles made out of three eggs, boil them fifteen minutes, drain, then mix with two tablespoons of fresh butter. Add some cinnamon and sugar to noodles. Put a layer of noodles, then apples and so on until pan is filled, being careful to have noodles on top. Put bits of fresh butter on top. Bake until apples are tender. If so desired, a milchig pie crust may be made and used as an under crust and when apples are tender and crust done, turn out on a large platter with crust side on top.

SCALLOPED NOODLES AND PRUNES

Make broad noodles with three eggs. Boil until tender, drain, pouring cold water through colander. Stew prunes, sprinkle with sugar and cinnamon. In a well-greased baking-dish place one-quarter of the noodles, bits of butter or other fat, add one-half of the prunes, then another layer of the noodles, butter or fat, the remaining prunes, the rest of the noodles. Pour over the prune juice and spread crumbs over top and bake in a moderate oven until crumbs are brown.

NOODLES AND MUSHROOMS

Make broad noodles, boil and serve with melted butter spread over the noodles and this sauce:

Brown a tablespoon of butter in the skillet, add one-half tablespoon of flour, then liquor of mushrooms, pinch of salt and pepper. When smooth, add mushrooms. Let boil and serve in a separate dish. When serving, a spoon of mushrooms is to be put over each portion of noodles.

GEROESTETE FERVELCHEN PFAeRVEL (EGG BARLEY)

Make just as you would a noodle dough, only stiffer, by adding and working in as much flour as possible and then grate on a coarse grater. Spread on a large platter to dry; boil one cup of egg barley in salt water or milk, which must boil before you put in the egg barley until thick. Serve with melted butter poured over them. (A simpler and much quicker way is to sift a cup or more of flour on a board; break in two eggs, and work the dough by rubbing it through your hands until it is as fine as barley grains.)

PFAeRVEL—FLEISCHIG

Make as much egg barley as required. Heat two tablespoons of fat, add one-quarter cup of onions, fry until golden brown, add the dried egg barley and brown nicely. Place in a pudding-dish, add three cups of hot soup stock or water to more than cover. Bake in a moderate oven about one hour or until the water has nearly all evaporated and the egg barley stands out like beads and is soft. The onion may be omitted. Serve hot in place of a vegetable.

KAESE KRAEPFLI (CHEESE KREPLICH)

Make a dough of one egg with a tablespoon of water; add a pinch of salt; work this just as you would noodle dough, quite stiff. Sift the flour in a bowl, break in the egg, add the salt and water, mix slowly by stirring with the handle of a knife, stirring in the same direction all the time. When this dough is so stiff that you cannot work it with the knife, flour your noodle board and work it with the hollow of your hands, always toward you, until the dough is perfectly smooth; roll out as thin as paper and cut into squares three inches in diameter. Fill with pot cheese or schmierkaese which has been prepared in the following manner: Stir up a piece of butter the size of an egg, adding one egg, sugar, cinnamon, grated peel of a lemon and pinch of salt, pounded almonds, which improve it; fill the kraepfli with a teaspoon, wet the edges with beaten egg, fold into triangles, pressing the edges firmly together; boil in boiling milk; when done they will swim to the top. Eat with melted butter or cream.

BOILED MACARONI

Break the macaroni into small pieces; boil for half an hour; drain and blanch in cold water. Reheat in tomato or cream sauce and serve. Grated cheese may be sprinkled over the dish if desired.

SPAGHETTI

Spaghetti is a small and more delicate form of macaroni. It is boiled until tender in salted water and is combined with cheese and with sauces the same as macaroni, and is usually left long. It makes a good garnish.

BAKED MACARONI WITH CHEESE

Cook one cup of broken macaroni in two quarts of boiling salted water for twenty or thirty minutes, drain and pour cold water through the colander. Put the macaroni in a pudding-dish in layers, covering each layer with cream sauce and grated cheese, one cup will be sufficient, and on the top layers sprinkle one cup of buttered bread crumbs. Bake in oven until the crumbs are brown.

SAVORY MACARONI

After baking; some flour to a pale fawn color pass it through a sieve or strainer to remove its gritty particles. Break half a pound of macaroni into short pieces, boil them in salted water until fairly tender, then drain.

In a little butter in a saucepan brown a level tablespoon of very finely chopped onion, then add three or four sliced tomatoes, a half teaspoon of powdered mixed herbs, a little nutmeg, salt and pepper. When the tomatoes are reduced to a pulp add one pint of milk and allow it to come to the boiling point before mixing with it two tablespoons of the browned flour moistened with water.

Stir and boil till smooth, press the whole through a strainer and return to the saucepan. When boiling, add the macaroni and a few minutes later stir in two tablespoons of grated or finely chopped cheese.

It may be served at once, but is vastly improved by keeping the pan for half an hour by the side of the fire in an outer vessel of water. Or the macaroni may be turned into a casserole and finished off in the oven.

For a meat meal the onions may be browned in sweet drippings or olive oil and soup stock substituted for the milk.

DUMPLINGS FOR STEW

Mix two teaspoons of baking powder with two cups of flour, one egg, one cup of cold water and a little salt.

Stir all lightly together and drop the batter from the spoon into the stew while the water continues to boil. Cover closely and do not uncover for twenty minutes, boiling constantly, but not too hard. Serve immediately in the stew.

SPAETZLEN OR SPATZEN

Sift two cups of flour into a bowl, make a depression in the centre and break into it two eggs, add a saltspoon of salt and enough water or milk to form a smooth, stiff dough. Set on some water to boil, salt the water and when the water boils drop the spaetzle into it, one at a time. Do this with the spoon with which you cut the dough, or roll it on a board into a round roll and cut them with a knife. When the spaetzle are done, they will rise to the surface, take them out with a perforated skimmer and lay them on a platter. Now heat two tablespoons of butter and add bread crumbs, let them brown for a minute and pour all over the spaetzle. If you prefer you may put the spaetzle right into the spider in which you have heated the butter. Another way to prepare them is after having taken them out of the water, heat some butter in a spider and put in the spaetzle, and then scramble a few eggs over all, stirring eggs and spaetzle together. Serve hot.

SOUR SPATZEN

Brown three tablespoons of flour with one tablespoon of sweet drippings, add a small onion finely chopped, then cover the spider and let the onion steam for a little while; do this over a low heat so there will be no danger of the union getting too brown; add vinegar and soup stock and two tablespoons of sugar. Let this boil until the sauce is of the right consistency. Serve with spaetzlen made according to the foregoing recipe, using water in place of the milk to form the dough. Pour the sauce over the spaetzlen before serving. By adding more sugar the sauce may be made sweet sour.

LEBERKNADEL (CALF LIVER DUMPLINGS)

Chop and pass through a colander one-half pound of calf's liver; rub to a cream four ounces of marrow, add the liver and stir hard. Then add a little thyme, one clove of garlic grated, pepper, salt and a little grated lemon peel, the yolks of two eggs and one whole egg. Then add enough grated bread crumbs or rolled crackers to this mixture to permit its being formed into little marbles. Drop in boiling salt water and let cook fifteen minutes; drain, roll in fine crumbs and fry in hot fat.

MILK OR POTATO NOODLES

Boil seven or eight potatoes, peel and let them stand several hours to dry; then grate them and add two eggs, salt and enough flour to make a dough thick enough to roll. Roll into long, round noodles as thick as two pencils and cut to length of baking-pan. Butter pan and lay noodles next to each other; cover with milk and lumps of butter and bake fifteen minutes, till yellow; serve immediately with bread crumbs browned in butter.

KARTOFFEL KLOESSE (POTATO DUMPLINGS)

Boil about eight potatoes in their jackets and when peeled lay them on a platter overnight. When ready to use them next day, grate, add two eggs, salt, a little nutmeg if desired, one wine-glass of farina, a tablespoon of chicken fat, one scant cup of flour gradually, and if not dry enough add more flour, but be sure not to make the mixture too stiff as this makes the balls heavy. Place balls in salted boiling water, cook until light and thoroughly done, serve just, as they are or fried in chicken fat until brown.

The dumplings may be made of the same mixture and in the centre of each dumpling place stripes of bread one inch long and one-fourth inch thick which have been fried in chicken fat and onions. Flour your hands well and make into dumplings. Put into boiling-salted water, boil about twenty-five minutes. Serve at once with chopped onions browned, or browned bread crumbs and chicken fat.

WIENER KARTOFFEL KLOESSE

Boil eight potatoes. When they are very soft drain off every drop of water, lay them on a clean baking-board and mash them while hot with a rolling-pin, adding about one cup of flour. When thoroughly mashed, break in two eggs, salt to taste, and flavor with grated nutmeg. Now flour the board thickly and foil out this potato dough about as thick as your little finger and spread with the following: Heat some fresh goose fat in a spider, cut up part of an onion very fine, add it to the hot fat together with one-half cup of grated bread crumbs. When brown, spread over the dough and roll just as you would a jelly-roll. Cut into desired lengths (about three or four inches), put them in boiling water, slightly salted, and boil uncovered for about fifteen minutes. Pour some hot goose grease over the dumplings.

BAIRISCHE DAMPFNUDELN, No. 1

Soak one cake of compressed yeast in a cup of lukewarm milk with a teaspoon of sugar, a teaspoon of salt, and sift a pint of flour in a bowl, in which you may also stir a small cup of milk and one egg. Pour in the yeast and work all thoroughly, adding more flour, but guarding against getting the dough too stiff. Cover up the bowl of dough and let it raise until it is as high again, which will take at least four hours. Flour a baking-board and mold small biscuits out of your dough, let them raise at least half an hour. Then butter a large, round, deep pan and set in your dumplings, brushing each with melted butter as you do so. When all are in, pour in enough milk to reach just half way up to the dumplings. Bake until a light brown. Eat hot, with vanilla sauce.

BAIRISCHE DAMPFNUDELN, No. 2

Make the dough just as you would in the above recipe, adding a tablespoon of butter, and after they have risen steam instead of baking them. If you have no steamer improvise one in this way: Put on a kettle of boiling water, set a colander on top of the kettle and lay in your dumplings, but do not crowd them; cover with a close-fitting lid and put a weight on top of it to keep in the steam, when done they will be as large again as when first put in. Take up one at first to try whether it is done by tearing open with two forks. If you have more than enough for your family, bake a pan of biscuits out of the remaining dough. Serve dumplings hot with prune sauce.

APPLE SLUMP

Pare, core and quarter apples, add a little water and sugar to taste, stew until tender and cover with the following mixture: Sift one pint of flour and one teaspoon of baking powder, add a pinch of salt and two cups of milk, mix and turn out onto a lightly floured board. Roll to one-half inch thickness and place over the stewed apples, cover and cook for ten minutes without lifting the lid. Serve hot with cream and sugar or soft custard.

BOILED APPLE DUMPLINGS

Beat well, without separating, two eggs, add a pinch of salt, two cups of milk and one cup of flour. To a second cup of flour, add two teaspoons of baking powder; add this to the batter and as much more flour as is necessary to make a soft dough. Roll out quickly one-half inch thick. Cut into squares, lay two or three quarters of pared apples on each, sprinkle with sugar and pinch the dough around the apples. Have a number of pudding cloths ready, wrung out of cold water, and sprinkle well with flour. Put a dumpling in each, leave a little room for swelling and tie tightly. Drop into a kettle of rapidly boiling water and keep the water at a steady boil for an hour. Serve hot with hard sauce.

Have a saucer in the bottom of kettle to prevent burning.

FARINA DUMPLINGS

Beat yolks of four eggs with three tablespoons of goose, turkey or chicken fat, but if these are not convenient, clear beef drippings will do. Put in enough farina to make a good Batter. Beat whites of eggs to a stiff froth with pinch of salt, and stir in batter. Put on in large boiler sufficient water to boil dumplings and add one tablespoon of salt. When boiling drop in by tablespoons. Boil one hour. This quantity makes twenty dumplings.

HUCKLEBERRY DUMPLINGS

Take a loaf of stale bread; cut off the crust and soak in cold water, then squeeze dry. Beat three eggs light, yolks and whites together add one quart berries and mix all together with a little brown sugar and a pinch of salt. Boil steadily one hour, serve with hard sauce.

PLUM KNOEDEL (HUNGARIAN)

Boil several potatoes, mash, mix with one egg yolk, a little salt and enough flour to make a dough soft enough to hold the impress of the finger. Roll out and cut into four-cornered pieces; in each square place a German plum which has had the pits removed and a mixture of sugar and cinnamon; put in place of the pit. Roll each square into a round dumpling; put these into a pan with boiling; salted water and let them cook covered for six or eight minutes. When done, serve with some bread crumbs browned in butter or schmalz and spread over the knoedel.

PEAR DUMPLING (BIRNE KLOESSE)

Take half a loaf of white bread or as much stale white bread, soak the white part and grate the crust, add one cup of suet chopped very fine, one cup of flour, one egg, salt and spices to taste, and one-half teaspoon of baking-powder. Make this into a dumpling, put it on a tiny plate in a large kettle. Lay prunes and pears around, about a pound of each, one cup of brown sugar, two pieces of stick cinnamon, dash of claret and cold water to almost cover; then cover kettle tightly and boil four hours. Serve hot.

Prunes and dried apples may be used as well.

PEACH DUMPLINGS

Make a dough of a quart of flour and a pint of milk, or water, a tablespoon of shortening, a pinch of salt, one egg and a spoon of sugar; add a piece of compressed yeast, which has previously been dissolved in water. Let the dough raise for three hours. In the meantime make a compote of peaches by stewing them with sugar and spices, such as cinnamon and cloves. Stew enough to answer for both sauce and filling. When raised, flour the baking-board and roll out the dough half an inch thick. Cut cakes out of it with a tumbler, brush the edges with white of egg, put a teaspoon of peach compote in the centre of a cake and cover it with another layer of cake and press the edges firmly together. Steam over boiling water and serve with peach sauce. A delicious dessert may also be made by letting the dough rise another half hour after being rolled out, and before cutting.

Compote of huckleberries may be used with these dumplings instead of peaches, if so desired.

CHERRY ROLEY-POLEY

Make a rich baking-powder biscuit dough, and roll it out until it is about two-thirds of an inch thick. Pit and stew enough cherries to make a thick layer of fruit and add sugar to taste. Spread them over the dough thickly and roll it up, taking care to keep the cherries from falling out. Wrap a cloth around it, and sew it up loosely with coarse thread, which is easily pulled out. Allow plenty of room for the dough to rise. Lay the roley-poley on a plate, set it in a steamer and steam for an hour and a half. Serve in slices, with cream or sauce.

SHABBAS KUGEL

Soak five wheat rolls in water, then press the bread quite dry, add one cup of drippings or one-half pound of suet chopped very fine, a pinch of salt, two eggs well beaten, one teaspoon of cinnamon, one grated lemon rind, one-half cup of sugar, one tablespoon of water. Stir all together thoroughly, grease the kugel pot well with warm melted fat, pour in the mixture and send it Friday afternoon to the bakery where it will remain till Saturday noon; it will then be baked brown. If one has a coal range that will retain the heat for the length of time required, it will be baked nicely. The kugel must be warm, however, when served.

KUGEL (SCHARFE)

If one desires an unsweetened kugel omit the sugar and cinnamon in the recipe above and season with salt and pepper. When required for any other meal but Shabbas, a kugel can be baked brown in two hours.

KUGEL

Soak five ounces of white bread—it may be stale bread—in cold water; then squeeze out every bit of water, put it in a bowl, add three-fourths cup of soft goose fat in small pieces, five whole eggs; one cup of flour, one-half cup of sugar, one-fourth cup of cracker meal, three apples and two pears cut in small pieces, two dozen raisins with the seeds removed, salt to taste, a tiny pinch of pepper, one-quarter teaspoon each of cinnamon and allspice. Mix all well together, and pour into an iron pan that has the bottom well covered with goose-fat; stick a few pieces of cut apple or pear in the top of the pudding. Pour a cup of cold water over all; place in the oven to bake. Bake slowly for five or six hours. If the water cooks out before it is ready to brown, add more. Bake brown, top and bottom.

NOODLE KUGEL

Cook three cups of broad noodles in salted boiling water ten minutes. Drain and add three-fourths cup of chicken or goose fat and four eggs, well beaten. Place in a well-greased iron pot and bake until the top of the kugel is well browned. Serve hot with raspberry jelly or stewed fruit of any kind.

PEAR KUGEL

Cream one cup of rendered fat with one cup of sugar, add one-half loaf of bread, previously soaked and pressed dry, a little salt, one-fourth cup of flour. Grease pudding-dish and put in alternate layers of the mixture and pears that have been boiled with water, sugar and claret. Bake slowly three hours.

KRAUT KUGEL

Chop up cabbage and let stew in fat slowly until quite brown. Do this the day previous to using. Next day mix in with the stewed cabbage one-fourth of a loaf of bread soaked in water and squeezed dry, one-half cup of flour, one-half cup of brown sugar, one-eighth pound of raisins, some finely chopped citron, one-fourth pound of almonds (mixed with a few bitter almonds), one-half teaspoon of salt, some cinnamon and allspice, about a teaspoon, juice and peel of one lemon and four eggs. Mix all thoroughly, pour into well-greased iron pan (kugel pot) and bake slowly.

APPLE KUGEL

Soak half a loaf of bread in water and squeeze dry, shave a cup of suet very fine and cut up some tart apples in thin slices. Add sugar, raisins, cinnamon, about one-quarter cup of pounded almonds and the yolks of three eggs. Mix all thoroughly. Add whites beaten to a stiff froth last. Bake one hour.

RICE KUGEL

Boil one cup of rice in water until done, then let it cool. In the meanwhile rub one-fourth cup of chicken-fat to a cream, add a scant cup of powdered sugar, a little cinnamon, the grated peel of one lemon, the yolks of three eggs, adding one at a time; one-half cup of raisins seeded, one-half pound of stewed prunes pitted, then add the cold rice. One-half cup of pounded almonds mixed with a few bitter ones improves this pudding. Serve with a pudding sauce, either wine or brandy. This pudding may be eaten hot or cold and may be either baked or boiled. If baked, one hour is required; if boiled, two hours; the water must be kept boiling steadily. Left-over rice may be used, butter instead of the fat, and the rice may be boiled in milk.

APPLE SCHALET, No. 1

Take one pound of fresh beef heart fat, shave it as fine as possible with a knife. Sift one quart of flour into a deep bowl, add two tumblers of ice-cold water, one tablespoon of brown sugar, a saltspoon of salt, then add the shaved heart fat and work well into the sifted flour. Put it on a pie-board and work as you would bread dough, with the palm of your hand, until it looks smooth enough to roll. Do not work over five minutes. Now take half of this dough, flour your pie-board slightly and roll out as you would pie dough, about once as thick. Grease a deep pudding-dish (an iron one is best), one that is smaller at the bottom than the top, grease it well, line the pudding-dish, bottom and sides, clear to the top, fill this one-third full with chopped tart apples, raisins, part of a grated lemon peel, citron cut quite fine, pounded almonds and melted drippings here and there. Sprinkle thickly with sugar, half brown and half white, and a little ground cinnamon. Moisten each layer with one-half wine-glass of wine. Now put another layer of dough, rolling out half of the remaining dough and reserving the other half for the top covering, fill again with apples, raisins, etc., until full, then put on top layer. Press the dough firmly together all round the edge, using a beaten egg to make sure of its sticking. Roll the side dough over the top with a knife and pour a cup of water over the pudding before setting it in the oven. Time for baking, two hours. If the top browns too quickly, cover.

This advantage of this pudding is, it may be baked the day previous to using, in fact, it is better the oftener it is warmed over—always adding a cup of water before setting it in the oven. Before serving the pudding turn it out carefully on a large platter, pour a wine-glass of brandy which has been slightly sweetened over the pudding and light it, carry to the table in flames. A novice had better try this pudding plain, omitting the wine, brandy, almonds and citron, moistening with water instead of wine before baking. Almost as nice and very good for ordinary use. Some apples require more water than others, the cook having to use her own judgment regarding the amount required.

APPLE SCHALET, No. 2

Line an iron pudding-dish with schalet dough, greasing it well before you do so. Chop up some apples quite fine, put on the crust, also some raisins (seeded), sugar and cinnamon, then put another layer of pie and another layer of chopped apples, and so on until filled, say about three layers, the last being crust. Bake slowly and long until a nice dark brown.

SCHALET DOUGH (MERBER DECK)

Cream four tablespoons of drippings, add a pinch of salt, two tablespoons of granulated sugar, beat in well one egg, add one cup of sifted flour and enough cold water to moisten dough so that it can be rolled out—about three tablespoons will be sufficient; it depends on the dryness of the flour how much is required.

NOODLE SCHALET

Make the quantity of noodles desired, then boil. When done, drain through colander, pouring cold water over the noodles.

When all the water has drained off, beat up three eggs in a large bowl, mix the noodles with the beaten eggs. Grease an iron pudding dish with plenty of goose grease or drippings, put in a layer of noodles, then sprinkle one-fourth cup of sugar, some pounded almonds, the grated peel of one lemon and a few raisins; sprinkle some melted fat over this, then add another layer of noodles, some more sugar and proceed as with the other layer until all the noodles are used. Bake two hours. Broad or fine noodles are equally good for this schalet. If desired, one tart apple chopped very fine may be added with the almonds.

CARROT SCHALET

Boil one pound of carrots, let them get perfectly cold before grating them. In the meanwhile cream a heaping tablespoon of drippings or chicken fat and four tablespoons of sugar, add gradually the yolks of four eggs, the grated peel of one lemon, one teaspoon of cinnamon, a little grated nutmeg, three tablespoons of flour, one teaspoon of baking-powder, pinch of salt, and the beaten whites last. Heat a few tablespoons of fat in a pudding dish, pour in the mixture and bake in a moderate oven one hour, then sprinkle sugar and cinnamon and return to oven for a few moments to brown. Serve hot.

SEVEN LAYER SCHALET

Take two cups of flour, one egg, three tablespoons of fat, one cup of water, a little sugar, pinch of salt, and knead lightly. Put dough aside in a cold place while you prepare a mixture of one cup of sugar, one and one-half teaspoons of cinnamon and three tablespoons of bread crumbs. Cut dough in seven pieces and roll out each piece separately. Place one layer on a greased baking-tin and spread the layer with melted fat and sprinkle with sugar and cinnamon; place upon this the second layer, sprinkle on this two ounces of sweet and bitter almonds which have been grated and mixed with sugar; over this place the third layer and spread with oil, sprinkle with cinnamon and sugar and one-half pound of cleaned, seedless raisins. Place the fourth layer on and spread with jelly and one-half pound of citron cut up very small. Cover over with another layer, spread fat and sprinkle with cinnamon and sugar and grated lemon peel and juice of lemon. Place the sixth layer and spread and sprinkle with sugar and cinnamon. Put on the last layer and spread with fat and sprinkle with sugar and cinnamon. Cut in four-cornered pieces and bake thoroughly and until a nice brown.

This schalet may be made and left whole; a frosting put on top and when well baked will keep for a month or more.

BOILED POTATO PUDDING

Stir the yolks of four eggs with one-half cup of sugar, add one-half cup of blanched and pounded almonds; grate in the peel, also the juice of one lemon, one-half pound of grated potatoes that have been boiled the day before. Lastly add the stiffly beaten whites, some salt and more potatoes, if necessary. Grease your pudding-pan well, pour in the mixture and bake. Set in a pan of water in oven; water in pan must not reach higher than one-half way up the pudding-form. Bake one-half hour. Turn out on platter and serve with a wine, chocolate, or lemon sauce. One can bake in an iron pudding-form without the water.

POTATO SCHALET

Peel and grate five or six large potatoes and one onion. Soak some bread and two or three crackers. Press out the water and add to the potatoes and onion, salt to taste. Add two tablespoons of boiling fat and one beaten egg. Have plenty of hot fat in pan, put in the pudding, pour over it one cup of cold water. Bake in hot oven one hour.

Two slices of white bread, one inch thick, will be sufficient bread for this schalet.

SWEET POTATO PUDDING

Take one quart of grated, raw sweet potatoes, one tablespoon leach of meat fat and chicken fat, one half pound of brown sugar, one-half pint of molasses, one and one-half pints of cold water, one saltspoon of salt and a little black pepper, grated orange peel, ginger, nutmeg and cinnamon to taste. Pour into greased baking-pan and bake until it jellies. Bake in moderate oven. May be eaten as a dessert, warm or cold.

APPLE STRUDEL, No. 1

Sift two cups of flour, add pinch of salt and one teaspoon of powdered sugar. Stir in slowly one cup of lukewarm water, and work until dough does not stick to the hands. Flour board, and roll, as thin as possible. Do not tear. Place a tablecloth on table, put the rolled out dough on it, and pull gently with the hands, to get the dough as thin as tissue paper.

Have ready six apples chopped fine, and mixed with cinnamon, sugar, one-half cup of seedless raisins, one-half cup of currants. Spread this over the dough with plenty of chicken-fat or oil all over the apples. Take the tablecloth in both hands, and roll the strudel, over and over, holding the cloth high, and the strudel will almost roll itself. Grease a baking-pan, hold to the edge of the cloth, and roll the strudel in. Bake brown, basting often with fat or oil.

APPLE STRUDEL, No. 2

Into a large mixing bowl place one and one-half cups of flour and one-quarter teaspoon of salt. Beat one egg lightly and add it to one-third cup of warm water and combine the two mixtures. Mix the dough quickly with a knife; then knead it, place on board, stretching it up and down to make it elastic, until it leaves the board clean. Now toss it on a well-floured board, cover with a hot bowl and keep in a warm place. While preparing the filling lay the dough in the centre of a well-floured tablecloth on the table; roll out a little, brush well with some melted butter, and with hands under dough, palms down, pull and stretch the dough gently, until it is as large as the table and thin as paper, and do not tear the dough. Spread one quart of sour apples, peeled and cut fine, one-quarter pound of almonds blanched and chopped, one-half cup of raisins and currants, one cup of sugar and one teaspoon of cinnamon, evenly over three-quarters of the dough, and drop over them a few tablespoons of melted butter. Trim edges. Roll the dough over apples on one side, then hold cloth high with both hands and the strudel will roll itself over and over into one big roll, trim edges again. Then twist the roll to fit the greased pan. Bake in a hot oven until brown and crisp and brush with melted butter. If juicy small fruits or berries are used, sprinkle bread crumbs over the stretched dough to absorb the juices. Serve slightly warm.

RAHM STRUDEL

Prepare the dough as for Apple Strudel as directed in the foregoing recipe, drip one quart of thick sour milk on it lightly, with a large spoon, put one cup of grated bread crumbs over the milk, add two cups of granulated sugar, one cup of chopped almonds, one cup of raisins, and one teaspoon of cinnamon, roll and place in well-buttered pan, put small pieces of butter over the top, basting frequently. Serve warm with vanilla sauce. One-half this quantity may be used for a small strudel.

CHERRY STRUDEL

Make a dough of two cups of flour, a pinch of salt and a little lukewarm water; do not make it too stiff, but smooth. Slap the dough back and forth. Do this repeatedly for about fifteen minutes. Now put the dough in a warm, covered bowl and set it in a warm, place for half an hour. In the meantime stem and pit two quarts of sour cherries. Grate into them some stale bread (about a plateful); also the peel of half a lemon, and mix. Add one cup of sugar, some ground cinnamon and about four ounces of pounded sweet almonds, mix all thoroughly. Roll out the dough as thin as possible, lay aside the rolling-pin and pull, or rather stretch the dough as thin as tissue paper. In doing this you will have to walk all around the table, for when well stretched it will cover more than the size of an ordinary table. Pull off all of the thick edge, for it must be very thin to be good (save the pieces for another strudel). Pour a little melted goose-oil or butter over this, and sprinkle the bread, sugar, almonds, cherries, etc., over it; roll the strudel together into a long roll. Have ready a long baking-pan well greased with either butter or goose-fat; fold the strudel into the shape of a pretzel. Butter or grease top also and bake a light brown; baste often while baking. Eat warm.

MANDEL (ALMOND) STRUDEL

Prepare the dough as for Apple Strudel No. 2. Blanch one-half pound of almonds and grind, when dried beat the yolks of four eggs light with one-quarter pound of granulated sugar, add the grated peel of one lemon and mix in the almonds. Spread over the dough with plenty of oil, butter or fat and roll. Bake; baste very often.

CABBAGE STRUDEL

Heat one-half cup of goose-fat, add one medium-sized cabbage and let it simmer until done, stirring constantly to keep from burning. While cooling prepare strudel dough, fill with cabbage and one cup of raisins and currants mixed, two cups of granulated sugar, one-half cup of chopped almonds and one teaspoon cinnamon, roll and put little pieces of grease on top; bake in hot oven and baste frequently. The pans in which the strudel is baked must be greased generously. Serve this strudel hot. This strudel may be made for a milk meal by substituting butter for fat.

QUARK STRUDEL (DUTCH CHEESE)

Make a strudel or roley-poley dough and let it rest until you have prepared the cheese. Take half a pound of cheese, rub it through a coarse sieve or colander, add salt, the yolks of two eggs and one whole egg, sweeten to taste. Add the grated peel of one lemon, two ounces of sweet almonds, and about four bitter ones, blanched and pounded, four ounces of sultana raisins and a little citron chopped fine. Now roll out as thin as possible, spread in the cheese, roll and bake, basting with sweet cream.

STRUDEL AUS KALBSLUNGE

Wash the lung and heart thoroughly in salt water, and put on to boil in cold water, adding salt, one onion, a few bay leaves and cook until very tender. Make the dough precisely the same as any other strudel. Take the boiled lung and heart, chop them as fine as possible and stew in a saucepan with some fat, adding chopped parsley, a little salt, pepper and mace, or nutmeg, the grated peel of half a lemon and a little wine. Add the beaten yolks of two eggs to thicken, and remove from the fire to cool. Roll out the dough as thin as possible, fill in the mixture and lay the strudel in a well-greased pan; put flakes of fat on top and baste often. Eat hot.

RICE STRUDEL

Prepare the dough same as for Apple Strudel. Leave it in a warm place covered, until you have prepared the rice. Wash a quarter of a pound of rice in hot water—about three times—then boil it in milk until very soft and thick. Let it cool, and then add two ounces of butter, the yolks of four eggs, four ounces of sugar and one teaspoon of vanilla, some salt and the beaten whites of two eggs, mix thoroughly. When your dough has been rolled out and pulled as thin as possible, spread the rice over it and roll. Add pounded almonds and raisins if desired. Put in a greased pan and bake until brown, basting with sweet cream or butter.

CEREALS

The cereals are the most valuable of the vegetable foods, including as they do the grains from which is made nearly all the bread of the world.

For family use, cereals should be bought in small quantities and kept in glass jars, tightly covered.

Variety is to be found in using the different cereals and preparing them in new ways. Many cereals are improved by adding a little milk during the latter part of the cooking. Boiling water and salt should always be added to cereals, one teaspoon salt to one cup of cereal. Long cooking improves the flavor and makes the cereal more digestible.

Cereals should be cooked the first five minutes over the fire and then over hot-water in a double boiler; if one cannot be procured, cook cereal in a saucepan set in a larger one holding the hot water.

LAWS ABOUT CEREALS

To discover if cereals such as barley, wheat, oats, farina or cornmeal are kosher, place them on a hot plate, if no worms or other insects appear they are fit to be eaten, if not, they must be thrown away.

If flour is mildewed it must be destroyed.

OATMEAL PORRIDGE

As oatmeal is ground in different grades of coarseness, the time for cooking varies and it is best to follow the directions given on the packages. The meal should be cooked until soft, but should not be mushy. The ordinary rule is to put a cup of meal into two cups of salted boiling water (a teaspoon of salt), and let it cook in a double boiler the required time. Keep covered until done; then remove the cover and let the moisture escape.

COLD OATMEAL

Oatmeal is very good cold, and in summer is better served in that way. It can be turned into fancy molds or into small cups to cool, and will then hold the form and make an ornamental dish.

OATMEAL WITH CHEESE

Cook one cup of oatmeal overnight and just before serving add one tablespoon of butter and one cup grated cheese. Stir until the cheese is melted and serve at once.

BAKED APPLE WITH OATMEAL

Pare and core the apples and fill the core space with left-over oatmeal mush. Put the apples in a baking dish; sprinkle with sugar; pour a little water into the bottom of the pan and bake in a moderate oven until the apples are tender. Serve warm with cream for breakfast or luncheon.

WHEAT CEREALS

Wheat cereals, like oatmeal, are best cooked by following the directions on the package. Most of them are greatly improved by the addition of a little milk or by a few chopped dates or whole sultana raisins.

CORNMEAL MUSH

Mix together one cup of cornmeal and one teaspoon of salt, and add one cup of cold water gradually, stirring until smooth. Pour this mixture into two cups of boiling; water in a double boiler and cook from three to five hours. Serve hot with cream and sugar.

SAUTED CORNMEAL MUSH

Put left-over mush into a dish and smooth it over the top. When cold cut into slices one-half inch thick. Dip each slice into flour. Melt one-half teaspoon of drippings in a frying-pan and be careful to let it get smoking hot. Brown the floured slices on each side. Drain if necessary and serve on a hot plate with syrup.

FARINA

To one-half cup of farina take one teaspoon of salt; pour gradually into three cups of boiling water and cook the mixture in a double boiler for about one hour.

HOMINY

Get the unbroken hominy and after careful washing soak it twenty-four hours in the water. Cook one cup of hominy slowly in the same water in a covered vessel for eight hours or until all the water has been absorbed by the hominy; add two tablespoons of butter, one teaspoon of salt and two tablespoons of cream and serve as a vegetable or as a cereal with sugar and cream.

MARMELITTA

Take two cups of coarse cornmeal and four cups of cold water put on to boil; add one-half teaspoon of salt. Stir the cornmeal continually and when done place on platter, spread with butter, sharf cheese or any cheese such as pot or cream cheese. To be eaten warm.

POLENTA

Place one cup of yellow cornmeal and three cups of cold water in a double boiler, add one teaspoon of salt, one-half teaspoon of pepper and cook for forty minutes. While still hot add one and one-half cups of grated cheese to the mixture and heat until it melts. Turn the mixture into a greased bowl and allow it to set. The meal may be sliced an inch thick or cut with a biscuit cutter and then fried in hot vegetable oil. Serve with white or tomato sauce as desired.

BARLEY, TAPIOCA, SAGO, ETC

Add one teaspoon of salt to one quart of boiling water and pour gradually on one-half cup of barley or other hard grain and boil until tender, from one to two or more hours, according to the grain, and have each kernel stand out distinct when done. Add more boiling water as it evaporates. Use as a vegetable or in soups. Pearl barley, tapioca and sago cook quicker than other large grains.

BOILED RICE

Put one-half cup of rice in a strainer; place the strainer over a bowl nearly full of cold water; rub the rice; lift the strainer from the bowl and change the water. Repeat this until the water in the bowl is clear. Have two quarts of water boiling briskly, add the rice and one tablespoon of salt gradually so as not to stop the boiling; boil twenty minutes or until soft, do not stir; drain through a colander and place the colander over boiling water for ten minutes to steam. Every grain will be distinct. Serve as a vegetable or as a cereal with cream and sugar.

RICE IN MILK

Clean the rice as for boiling in water; and cook one-half cup of rice with one and one-half cups of hot milk and one-half teaspoon of salt, adding a few seeded or sultana raisins if desired. Serve hot like boiled rice or press into small cups, cool and serve with cream and sugar.

RICE WITH GRATED CHOCOLATE

Cook one-half cup of rice, place in hot serving dish, sprinkle generously with grated sweet chocolate; set in oven one minute and serve.

STEAMED RICE

Wash two cups of rice carefully put in double boiler; add eight cups of cold water and a pinch of salt and steam for two hours; do not stir. Serve with any kind of stewed fruit or preserve.

APPLES WITH RICE

Boil one cup of rice in water or milk; rub the kettle all over with a piece of butter before putting in the rice, season with salt and add a lump of butter. When cooked, add about six apples, pared, quartered and cored, sugar and cinnamon. This makes a nice side dish, or dessert, served with cream.

BOILED RICE WITH PINEAPPLE

Boil as much rice as desired and when done slice up the pineapple and add, with as much sugar as is required to sweeten to taste.

BAKED RICE

Arrange two cups of boiled rice in a baking dish in layers, covering each with grated cheese, a little milk, butter, salt and red pepper. Spread one cup of grated bread crumbs over all and bake in a moderate oven until the crumbs are browned.

SWEET RICE

Clean and wash one cup of rice. Put on to boil with cold water, add a pinch of salt. When done drain off the water, if any; add two cups of milk, stir in and let boil for five minutes. Dish up, then sprinkle sugar and cinnamon generously over the top. The yolk of an egg can be added just before serving if desired.

EGGS BAKED IN RICE

Line a buttered dish with steamed rice. Break the eggs in the centre, dot with butter, sprinkle with salt, pepper and bake in a moderate oven.

RICE AND NUT LOAF

Boil one-half cup of rice (brown preferred); drain and dry it. Mix with an equal quantity of bread crumbs. Add level teaspoon of salt and one-half saltspoon of black pepper. Stir in one cup of chopped nuts—pecans or peanuts. Add one tablespoon of chopped parsley and one egg. Mix thoroughly and pack in bread-pan to mold it. Turn it from pan into baking-pan and bake slowly three-quarters of an hour. Serve with cream sauce or puree of peas.

PILAF

Put two cups of water on to boil, add juice of two tomatoes and a pinch of salt. When boiling, add one cup of rice and let cook until the water has evaporated. Then add melted butter, mix well, and keep in warm place, covered, until ready to serve.

SPANISH RICE

Put one cup of washed rice in frying-pan with four or five tablespoons of poultry fat; add three onions chopped and two cloves of garlic minced fine. Fry ten minutes; add one red pepper or one canned pimento chopped, or one teaspoon of paprika, and three ripe tomatoes or two cups of strained tomatoes and one teaspoon of salt. Cook slowly about one hour, and as the water evaporates, add more boiling water to keep from burning.

LEFT-OVER CEREALS

Oatmeal, hominy, cracked wheat, and other cereals which are left over can be added next day to the fresh stock, for they are improved by long boiling and do not injure the new supply, or such as is left can be molded in large or in small forms, and served cold with cream, or milk and sugar. In warm weather cereals are nicer cold than hot. Cold hominy and mush, cut into squares and fried, so that a crisp crust is formed on both sides,—also hominy or farina, rolled into balls and fried,—are good used in place of a vegetable or as a breakfast dish.

Any of the cereals make good pancakes, or a small amount added to the ordinary pancake batter improves it.

EGGS

Eggs and the foods into which they enter are favorite articles of diet in most households. They are an agreeable substitute for meat and even when high in price make a cheaper dish than meat.

A fresh egg should feel heavy, sink in water, and when held to a bright light show a clear round yolk.

TO PRESERVE EGGS

In the early spring or fall when eggs are plentiful and at their best, pack them away for future use. Use strictly fresh eggs with perfect shells (no cracks). Buy water glass at drugstore. Use ten parts water to one of water glass. Boil water, when cool add water glass and beat well. Use an earthen jar or crock, pack in rows and pour over the liquid mixture to cover well. Place old plate over eggs in crock to keep them under water. Put cover on jar and keep in cool place. More eggs may be added at any time if well covered with the liquid mixture.

For fifteen dozen eggs use one quart water glass.

TO KEEP EGG YOLKS

The yolks may be kept several days and be as if just separated from the whites if they are placed in a cup previously rinsed with cold water and a pinch of salt added to them. The cup must be closely covered with a wet cloth, and this must be changed and well rinsed in cold water every day.

When whites are left over make a small angel cake or any of the cookies which require the whites of egg only.

When yolks are left over use for making mayonnaise.

POACHED OR DROPPED EGGS

Fill a pan with boiling, salted water. Break each egg into a wet saucer and slip it into the water; set the pan back where water will not boil. Dip the water over the eggs with a spoon. When the white is firm and a film has formed over the yolk, they are cooked. Take them up with a skimmer, drain and serve hot, on toast. Season with salt.

BOILED EGGS

Soft-boiled eggs may be prepared in two ways. The eggs may be dropped carefully into boiling water and boiled three minutes, or they may be placed in a covered vessel of boiling water and allowed to stand in a warm place (but not on the stove) for ten minutes. Eggs prepared in this way are sometimes called "Coddled Eggs." They are much more delicate and digestible than the usual "Boiled Eggs."

Hard-boiled eggs should be cooked in boiling water for fifteen or twenty minutes and then dropped in cold water to prevent the yolk from turning dark.

SCRAMBLED EGGS

Break into a bowl as many eggs as required, add salt and pepper. Have some very hot butter in the frying-pan on the stove; pour in the eggs, stir constantly until set, not stiff, and serve on a hot platter at once.

FRIED EGGS

Melt in a frying-pan a piece of butter, or fat for a meat meal. When hot, drop in the eggs, one at a time, being careful not to break the yolk. When the white of the egg is set they are done, though some persons like them turned over and cooked on the other side. Remove from the pan with a cake turner.

BAKED EGGS

Butter individual baking dishes and break an egg in each, being careful to keep the yolk whole. Put on each egg a bit of butter, a little pepper and salt. Bake in moderate oven from four to six minutes.

BAKED EGGS WITH CHEESE

Butter a baking dish of a size necessary for number of eggs desired, break eggs into dish, add salt, paprika, pepper to taste, one tablespoon of cream, and two tablespoons of grated cheese.

Place dish in a pan of hot water in moderate oven for five minutes until eggs are set.

TOMATO WITH EGG

Cut top from tomatoes, remove seeds, put a raw egg in each tomato, dust with salt, pepper, and finely chopped parsley. Place in moderate oven until egg is set. Serve with cream sauce.

BAKED EGG WITH TOMATOES

Remove the skin from six fresh tomatoes or take one-half can of tomatoes, chop them and put them on stove and cook for twenty minutes; season with one tablespoon of chopped parsley, half an onion chopped, salt and pepper; thicken at the end of that time with one teaspoon of melted butter mixed with one tablespoon of flour. Put aside to cool. Then mix in the yolks of four eggs well beaten, and lastly cut and fold in the four whites. Butter a pudding dish and set this mixture in the oven in a pan of lukewarm water and bake in a moderate oven until a golden brown.

PLAIN OMELET

To make an omelet for breakfast or luncheon for two persons, take three eggs, three tablespoons of sweet milk and a saltspoon of salt. Whip the yolks of the eggs, the milk and salt to a light foam with an egg whip. Slowly add the yolk mixture to the whites of the eggs, which should be beaten to a stiff froth in a big bowl. After the yolks and milk are well whipped through the whites, beat the whole together for a few minutes with the egg-beater.

In an omelet pan or a large frying-pan put a tablespoon of good butter. When the butter is bubbling hot, pour in the omelet mixture. Stir it lightly for the first minute with a broad-bladed knife, then stop stirring it; and, as the mixture begins to stiffen around the edge, fold the omelet toward the centre with the knife. As soon as it is properly folded, turn it over on a hot platter. Decorate with sprigs of parsley and serve.

SWEET OMELET

Six eggs, two tablespoons of flour, one cup of cold milk. Wet the flour with a little of the milk, then add the rest of the milk and the yolks of the eggs. Beat the whites of the eggs to a stiff froth and pour into the flour, milk and yolks. Put a piece of butter into a spider and let it get hot, but not so hot that the butter will burn. Then pour the mixture in and put in a moderate oven to bake in the spider. It takes about ten minutes to bake. Then slip a knife under it and loosen it and slip off on a large plate. Sift powdered sugar on top and serve with a slice of lemon.

SWEET OMELET FOR ONE

One egg, beat white separately, two tablespoons of cold sweet milk, a pinch of salt. Brown on both sides or roll, spread with compote or sprinkle powdered sugar thickly over it. Serve at once.

SPANISH OMELET

In a chopping bowl place two nice large ripe tomatoes, first peeling them; one large or two medium-sized white Texas onions, two sprigs of parsley, and one large green-bell pepper, first removing most of its seeds.

Chop these ingredients well together quite fine, turn them into a saucepan and let them cook over rather a brisk heat until quite soft. Put no water in this mixture. Add a tablespoon of olive oil or of butter before it begins to cook and season well with salt and red pepper.

Make the omelet the same as the plain one, but use water instead of milk in mixing it, and only use two tablespoons of water for the six eggs required.

After the eggs are sufficiently beaten, mixed, and in the pan over the fire, and when the edges begin to stiffen, cover the surface of the omelet to within an inch of the edge with the cooked vegetables. Fold the omelet quickly and turn it on a hot platter. Pour around it all the vegetables left in the pan and serve.

RUM OMELET

Take six eggs, beat whites and yolks well, add a pinch of salt and a teaspoon of brandy. Fry in a spider quickly and spread with a compote of huckleberries or any other fruit. Roll up the omelet, pour a very small wineglass of rum over it, light it and serve at once.

SWEET ALMOND OMELET

Prepare one-half cup of sweet almonds, blanched, chopped fine and pounded smooth. Beat four eggs slightly, add four tablespoons of cream and turn it into a hot omelet pan on which you have melted one tablespoon, of butter. Cook carefully, drawing the cooked portion into the centre and tilting the pan to allow the liquid part to run over the bare pan. When nearly all set, sprinkle the almonds over the surface and turn the edges over until well rolled. Then slip it out on a hot dish and dredge with powdered sugar, and scatter several salted almonds over the top. Serve immediately.

CORN OMELET

Take one-half cup of canned corn and chop it very fine (or the same amount cut from the cob). Add to that the yolk of one egg, well beaten with pepper and salt to taste, and two tablespoons of cream. Beat the white of the egg very stiff and stir in just before cooking. Have the pan very hot and profusely buttered. Pour the mixture on, and when nicely browned, turn one half over the other, as in cooking other omelets.

HERB OMELET

Take six eggs and beat well in a bowl. Add two tablespoons of cold water and a quarter of a teaspoon of salt, a pinch of pepper, a teaspoon of chopped parsley, a quarter of a teaspoon of grated onion and a teaspoon of fine butter, shaved in little pieces. Mix well with a wooden spoon. Dissolve in the spider the butter and add at once the beaten eggs, etc., inclining the spider to the handle for an instant and then shaking the omelet into the centre and turn up the right edge, then the left and fry briskly five minutes and serve.

POACHED EGGS WITH FRIED TOMATOES

Fry tomatoes (cut one-half inch thick) in butter, pepper and salt. Have prepared slices of bread cut round, and fried in butter. Put on a hot platter with a slice of tomato on each. Poach as many eggs as are required, in boiling salt water. Lift out very carefully, placing one egg on each tomato. Add to the gravy in which tomatoes were fried, two tablespoons of cream, one teaspoon of any pungent sauce, one teaspoon of mushroom catsup, juice of half a lemon, and a teaspoon of flour to thicken. Cook up once and pour over eggs. Serve very hot.

EGGS POACHED IN TOMATO SAUCE

Make a sauce of one tablespoon of butter, one tablespoon of flour, one and one-half cups of canned tomatoes rubbed through a strainer, a pinch of soda, salt, pepper and sugar to taste. When sufficiently cooked drop in the required number of eggs, cook until the white is firm, basting the eggs often with the sauce. When done, lift the eggs carefully to squares of toast and pour the sauce around them.

EGGS PIQUANT

Set to boil the following mixture: Pour into the kettle water to the depth of about one inch, adding a little salt and half a cup of vinegar. When this boils, break in as many fresh eggs, one at a time, as you desire to have. Do this carefully so as not to break the yolks. As soon as the whites of the eggs are boiled, take up carefully with a perforated skimmer and lay in cold water. Then remove to a large platter and pour over the following sauce: Strain the sauce the eggs were boiled in and set away until you have rubbed or grated two hard-boiled eggs, yolks only. Add a tablespoon of butter rubbed very hard and add also some sugar and part of the strained sauce. Boil up once and pour over the eggs. Garnish with parsley.

OMELET SOUFFLE

Yolks of six eggs and six tablespoons of powdered sugar, added gradually, and both beaten together until thick and smooth; juice of one lemon and a little grated rind; whites beaten as stiff as possible, stirred together. Put into a warm well-buttered dish; bake in quick oven ten minutes.

WHITE SAUCE OMELET

Make a white sauce of one tablespoon of butter blended with two tablespoons of flour, one-half teaspoon of salt, pinch of pepper and one teaspoon of sugar, adding one-half cup each of milk and cream. Beat the yolks of five eggs and stir them into the sauce, then add the stiffly beaten whites of the eggs, folding them in carefully. Melt two tablespoons of butter in the omelet pan, when it is hot put in the mixture and let it stand in a moderate heat for two minutes, place in a hot oven and cook until set. Remove from the oven, turn on a hot platter and serve.

EGGS WITH CREAM DRESSING

Blend two tablespoons of butter with three tablespoons of flour. Place on range and stir until the butter is melted. Add one and one-half cups of milk, stirring all the time until the mixture is thick; season with one teaspoon of salt and a few grains of pepper. Separate the whites of six hard-boiled eggs from the yolks. Chop the whites fine and add to the dressing. Arrange slices of toast on a hot platter, pour the dressing over them; force the yolks through a ricer onto the toast and dressing; serve hot.

SCALLOPED EGGS

Use above recipe and mix one cup of bread crumbs with one tablespoon of butter, sprinkle this over dish and bake fifteen minutes in a hot oven.

EGGS A LA MEXICANA

Boil six dried Spanish peppers twenty minutes. Drain, remove the seeds, and chop fine. Fry in butter half an onion and one clove of garlic. Add one cup of uncooked rice, cover with one cup of water and cook till tender. Add a lump of butter, salt, and, when done, cover with six eggs; then scramble all together. Serve on a hot dish.

EGGS SPANISH

Boil eggs hard; after cooling, remove shells and halve lengthwise. Cook for thirty minutes fresh or canned tomatoes with minced green onions, garlic, parsley, a laurel leaf, salt, pepper, and cayenne pepper to taste. Strain. Melt a slice of butter, add a little flour, and then add sauce gradually. Cook ten minutes; place eggs carefully in sauce and serve.

FRESH MUSHROOMS WITH EGGS

Peel nine good-sized mushrooms without using the stems and chop very fine; fry two tablespoons of butter and two finely chopped onions without browning. Add the mushrooms and steam them by covering the pan after seasoning with salt, pepper and paprika. Before serving, beat six whole eggs and scramble with the mushrooms. Serve on hot buttered toast.

EGG RAREBIT

Make a cream sauce. Grate one-half pound American and Swiss cheese mixed, or American alone; add to the sauce. Chop three hard-boiled eggs, add to the sauce, season with salt and pepper, and serve on buttered toast.

KROSPHADA

Place two sliced onions with two ounces each of sugar and spices, pepper and salt to taste, in a pint of pure malt vinegar and boil gently until the onions are nearly done. Let it cool a little and then stir in six beaten eggs and sufficient crumbled ginger-bread to make the whole quite thick. Place again over the fire for a few minutes, stirring frequently and mashing the mixture into a uniform paste, but be very careful that it does not boil.

CURRIED EGGS

Melt four tablespoons of butter in a frying-pan, add one onion chopped fine and cook until straw colored. Then add one tablespoon of curry powder. Make a smooth paste of one-fourth of a cup of water and two tablespoons of flour; add one tablespoon of lemon juice and one-half teaspoon of salt. Add to the first mixture; boil five minutes. Arrange six hard-boiled eggs in a border of rice and pour the dressing over all.

FRICASSEED EGGS

Take six hard-boiled eggs, remove shells. Roll them in flour, then in egg to which has been added one-half teaspoon of oil, one-half teaspoon of vinegar, a few drops of onion juice, one teaspoon chopped parsley, a little nutmeg and salt. When quite covered, roll in vermicelli that has been broken into fine bits and fry in deep beef drippings. Serve with the following sauce: One tablespoon of fat; one tablespoon of flour, browned together; add one-half cup of white wine and a cup of bouillon. Season with salt and cayenne and boil five minutes. Add one teaspoon each of chopped chives and parsley, some chopped olives and mushrooms; bring to a boil again and pour over the eggs.

EGGS EN MARINADE

Mix equal quantities of water and good meat gravy, two tablespoons each, with a teaspoon of vinegar and a seasoning of pepper and salt. Put in a stew-pan and stir in gradually two well-beaten, yolks of eggs. When it thickens and before it boils, have ready a half dozen nicely poached eggs and pour the sauce over them. Garnish with parsley.

SCALLOPED EGGS (FLEISCHIG)

Make a force-meat of chopped tongue, bread crumbs, pepper, salt, a little parsley, one tablespoon of melted fat, and soup stock enough to make a soft paste. Half fill patty-pans with the mixture. Break an egg carefully on the top of each, sprinkle with a little salt, pepper and cracker dust. Put in the oven and bake about ten minutes. Serve hot.

SCRAMBLED EGGS WITH BRAINS

Scald brains with hot water, clean and skin, and boil a few minutes in fresh water. Melt a little fat in skillet, put in brains, finely chopped, and stir well until dry and done. Add one teaspoon of chopped parsley, pinch of salt, and three eggs well-beaten. Stir with a fork until eggs are evenly cooked, put on hot platter, and serve immediately.

SCRAMBLED EGGS WITH SAUSAGE

Take one pound of cold, boiled sausage, skin and slice in half-inch pieces. Place in a frying-pan with two tablespoons of hot fat; brown on both sides a few minutes and just before serving add three eggs, beaten slightly; mix; and cook until the eggs are set and serve immediately.

Chopped tongue root may be used instead of sausage.

SMOKED BRISKET OF BEEF AND EGGS

Take slices of smoked breast of beef, brown in frying-pan; place on hot platter. Slip as many eggs as are needed in frying-pan and cook gently by dripping the hot fat over them until done. Place carefully on the beef slices and serve at once.

CHEESE

Cheese should not be tightly covered. When it becomes dry and hard, grate and keep covered until ready to use. It may be added to starchy foods.

Care should be exercised in planning meals in which cheese is employed as a substitute for meat. As cheese dishes are inclined to be somewhat "heavy," they should be offset by crisp, watery vegetables, water cress, celery, lettuce, fruit salads and light desserts, preferably fresh or cooked fruit. Another point, too, is to be considered. Whether raw or cooked, cheese seems to call for the harder kinds of bread—crusty rolls or biscuits, zwieback, toast, pulled bread or hard crackers.

A soft, crumbly cheese is best for cooking.

Cheese is sufficiently cooked when melted, if cooked longer it becomes tough and leathery.

Baking-soda in cheese dishes which are cooked makes the casein more digestible.

COTTAGE CHEESE (POT CHEESE)

Heat sour milk slowly until the whey rises to the top; pour it off, put the curd in a bag and let it dry for six hours without squeezing it. Pour it into a bowl and break it fine with a wooden spoon. Season with salt. Mold into balls and keep in a cool place. It is best when fresh.

KOCH KAESE (BOILED CHEESE)

Press one quart of fine cottage cheese through a coarse sieve or colander and set it away in a cool place for a week, stirring it once or twice during that time; when it has become quite strong, stir it smooth with a wooden or silver spoon; add a saltspoon of salt and one-fourth as much of caraway seed, yolks of two eggs and an even tablespoon of flour which has been previously dissolved in about one-half cup of cold milk; stir the flour and milk until it is a smooth paste, adding a lump of butter, about the size of an egg; add all to the cheese. Put the cheese on to boil until quite thick; stirring occasionally; boil altogether about one-half hour, stirring constantly the last ten minutes; the cheese must look smooth as velvet. Pour it into a dish which has been previously rinsed in cold water. Set it away in a cool place; to keep it any length of time, cover it with a clean cloth which has been dipped in and wrung out of beer. This cheese is excellent for rye bread sandwiches.

A DELICIOUS CREAM CHEESE

Sweet milk is allowed to stand until it is like a jelly, but does not separate. Then it is poured into a cheese-cloth bag and hung up to drain until all the water is out of it and only the rich creamy substance remains. Sometimes it takes from twelve to twenty-four hours. At the end of this time the cheese is turned from the bag into a bowl; then to every pint of the cheesy substance a tablespoon of butter is added and enough salt to season it palatably. Then it is whipped up with a fork until it is a smooth paste and enough put on a plate to make a little brick, like a Philadelphia cheese. With two knives, one in each hand, lightly press the cheese together in the shape of a brick, smooth it over the top and put it away to cool. One quart of rich sour milk will make a good sized cheese.

CHEESE BALLS, No. 1

Take one cake of cream cheese, one-quarter of a pound of chopped figs, one-quarter of a pound of chopped walnuts, roll into balls and serve on lettuce leaves.

CHEESE BALLS, No. 2

Mix one cake Neufchatel cheese, a piece of butter the size of the cheese, one tablespoon of cream, one-quarter teaspoon of salt and six dashes of Tabasco Sauce and form one large ball or several small ones and roll in chopped pecan nuts.

CHEESE SOUFFLE

Dissolve one and one-half tablespoons of butter, add one tablespoon of flour, stir until it loosens from the pan; add one and one-half cups of rich milk, pepper and salt. Take from the fire, add gradually four egg yolks and three-quarters of a cup of grated cheese, then the stiffly beaten whites of eggs. Bake in a hot oven in china ramekins about fifteen minutes and serve immediately.

CHEESE TIMBALS FOR TWELVE PEOPLE

Take one pint of milk, four tablespoons of flour, and use enough of the milk to dissolve the flour, the balance put in double boiler; when it boils, add the dissolved flour, then add one-quarter pound imported Swiss cheese grated. Let these two boil for fifteen minutes; when cool, add the yolks of four eggs; drop one in at a time and beat, then strain through a fine sieve about ten minutes before you put in the pans; beat the whites of two eggs and put in the above and mix; grease timbal forms, fill three-quarters full only; bake in pan of boiling water twenty minutes. Let them stand about two minutes, turn out on little plates, and serve with tomato sauce, a sprig of parsley put on top of each one.

WELSH RAREBIT

Melt one tablespoon of butter, add two cups finely cut American cheese, when it melts add one-half cup of milk or stale beer, keep stirring until it is smooth. Add one-half teaspoon of English mustard, two beaten eggs. Cook one minute longer and salt to taste. Serve on toast.

GOLDEN BUCK

One pound of cheese, one-eighth pound of butter, one-half glass of ale, one teaspoon of mustard, one egg (well beaten), and salt and paprika. Put butter in pan, and when melted add cheese cut up or grated; stir, and as cheese melts, add ale. When it begins to bubble, add egg well beaten. Stir continually to keep from getting stringy. In two or three minutes it will be ready to serve. Pour over hot buttered toast. This quantity is sufficient for four persons.

CHEESE BREAD

Take six thick slices of stale bread, well buttered; cut them in two; dip into milk; then place in a baking dish, with alternating layers of thinly sliced cheese, having cheese for top. Add half a cup of milk, into which a half teaspoon of dry mustard has been put. Bake in quick oven fifteen minutes. Serve at once.

GREEN CORN, TOMATOES AND CHEESE

Into one tablespoon of melted butter stir two cups of grated cheese until it, too, is melted. Add three-quarters of a cup of canned or grated fresh corn, one ripe green pepper, stir them, add one egg yolk mixed with one-half cup of tomato puree, one teaspoon of salt, one-half teaspoon of paprika. Toast five slices of bread and pour this mixture over it. Serve hot.

RICE AND CHEESE

Melt two ounces of butter in a stew-pan; fry in the buttery finely minced onion. When this is of a nice golden color stir into it a quarter of a pound of well-boiled rice. Work it well with a fork and then pour all into a buttered pie dish. Dredge over with a good coating of grated cheese, sprinkle the surface with melted butter and bake until nicely browned.

MACARONI AND CHEESE

Break three ounces of macaroni—noodles or spaghetti answer equally well—into small pieces, boil in rapidly boiling salted water; when tender drain off the water and add half a pint of milk; cook slowly till the macaroni has absorbed most of the milk. To half a pint of thick white sauce add two ounces of grated cheese and mix with the macaroni; last of all add two well-beaten eggs. Butter a pudding mold, sprinkle it with browned bread crumbs and pour in the macaroni mixture; steam gently for about half an hour, turn out and fill the centre with stewed tomatoes and mushrooms.

CHEESE OMELET

Cook in double boiler one cup of milk, add one tablespoon of butter, one tablespoon of flour blended together and cook till thick; one cup of cheese cut up added, and stir till dissolved. Remove from fire and stir in yolks of four eggs beaten, one-half teaspoon of salt (pepper). Fold in whites of four eggs beaten stiff and a pinch of baking powder. Bake in a buttered dish one-half hour.

CHEESE AND SWEET GREEN PEPPERS

Cheese and peppers make a very nice combination. Melt two ounces of cheese, add a tablespoon of chopped peppers and the same amount of butter, a little paprika, salt, and if liked, mustard. When the ingredients have been well blended pour the mixture on hot buttered toast and serve.

CHEESE FONDUE

Soak one-half cup of bread crumbs in one scant cup of milk; dissolve a speck of bicarbonate of soda in a drop of hot water and add to the milk, one egg, yolk and white beaten separately, one-half cup of dry cheese grated, one tablespoon of butter, salt and pepper to taste, beat well, pour into a well buttered baking dish, strew dry crumbs moistened with butter over the top, and bake in a hot oven until light brown. Serve at once in the dish in which it is baked.

TOMATOES, EGGS AND CHEESE (HUNGARIAN STYLE)

Place two tablespoons of butter in a pan (after having the water boil to heat the pan). Let butter melt, add one small onion chopped fine and cook until soft, a pint of tomatoes strained and let come to a boil; add one-half pound mild cheese cut fine; and stir until smooth. Break in three eggs and stir hard until eggs are done. Serve on buttered toast.

CRACKERS AND CHEESE

Split in two some Bent's water biscuits; moisten them with hot water and pour over each piece a little melted butter and French mustard; then spread with a thick layer of grated cheese; sprinkle with paprika or cayenne.

Place them in a hot oven until the cheese is soft and creamy.

RAMEKINS OF EGG AND CHEESE

Beat three new-laid eggs and blend thoroughly with two ounces of grated cheese and one ounce of partly melted butter. Place the mixture in little pans or saucers and bake in the oven.

BREAD

Home-made bread is very much more palatable and more nutritious than baker's bread and it is worth while to spend time and effort in its preparation.

To make good bread, it is necessary to have good flour, fresh yeast and the liquid used in moistening must be neither too hot nor too cold or the bread will not rise properly.

FLOUR

The housekeeper should know about the different kinds of flour. We get the bread flour from the spring wheat; the pastry flour from the winter wheat.

Bread flour contains more gluten than pastry flour and is used for bread on that account. Pastry flour having less gluten and slightly more starch is more suitable for pastry and cake mixtures and is used wherever softness and lightness are desired.

Graham flour is the whole kernel of wheat ground.

Entire wheat flour is the flour resulting from the grinding of all but the outer layer of the wheat.

Rye flour is next best to wheat flour for bread making, but is generally combined with wheat flour, since by itself it makes a sticky bread.

Cornmeal is also combined with wheat flour.

Variety bread is composed of bread flour, rye flour and cornmeal combined in one loaf.

If flour is musty; it is not kosher and must be destroyed. Keep flour either in tins or barrels in a dry atmosphere.

YEAST

In cities where fresh compressed yeast can be obtained, it is not worth while to prepare one's own.

Compressed yeast is always in proper condition to use until it becomes soft, often the yeast cakes are slightly discolored, but this does not affect the yeast, being caused by the oxidation of the starch in the cake.

Keep yeast in cool place.

HOME MADE YEAST

Grate six large raw potatoes, have ready a gallon of water in which you have boiled one and one-half cups of hops. Strain through a fine hair sieve, boiling hot, over the potatoes, stirring well, or the mixture will thicken like starch. Add a scant cup of sugar and one-half cup of salt. When cold, add a yeast cake or a cup of fresh yeast. Let it stand until a thick foam rises on the top. Bottle in a few days. If kept in a cool place, this yeast will last a long time. Use one cup of yeast for one large baking. In making yeast, from time to time, use a cup of the same with which to start the new yeast.

One cup of liquid yeast is equal to one cake of compressed yeast.

When yeast is not obtainable to start the fermentation in making yeast, mix a thin batter of flour and water, and let it stand in a warm place until it is full of bubbles. This ferment has only half the strength of yeast so double the amount must be used.

TO MAKE BREAD

Try the yeast always by setting to raise in a cup of lukewarm water or milk, if you use compressed yeast add salt and sugar.

If it rises in the course of ten or fifteen minutes, the yeast is fit to use. In making bread always use sifted flour. Set a sponge with lukewarm milk or water, keeping it covered in a warm place until very light, then mold this sponge by adding flour, until very light into one large ball, then knead well and steadily for twenty minutes. Set to rise again in a warm place free from drafts, and when it has risen to double its former bulk, take a knife, cut through the dough in several places, then place this dough on a baking board which has been sprinkled with flour. Work with the palm of the hand, always kneading towards the centre of the ball (the dough must rebound like a rubber ball). When this leaves the board and the hands perfectly clean the dough may be formed into loaves or rolls.

Place in pan, greased slightly with a good oil, let rise until the imprint of the finger does not remain, and bake.

The oven for baking bread should be hot enough to brown a teaspoon of flour in five minutes.

If baked in a coal range, the fire must be just the proper heat so as not to have to add fuel or shake the stove.

If baked in a gas range, light oven to full heat five minutes before putting the bread in the oven, and bake in a moderately hot oven forty-five minutes, unless the loaves are very large when one hour will be the proper time.

When taken from the oven, the bread may be wrapped in a clean towel wrung out of warm water (this prevents the crust from becoming hard); place bread in slanting position or allow it to cool on a wire rack.

WHITE BREAD

Set the dough at night and bake early in the morning; take one-half cake of compressed yeast, set in a cup of lukewarm milk or water adding a teaspoon of salt and a tablespoon of sugar. Let this rise, if it does not, the yeast is not fresh or good. Measure eight cups of sifted flour into a deep bread bowl, add one teaspoon of salt; make a depression in the centre, pour in the risen yeast and one cup of lukewarm milk or water. In winter be sure that the bowl, flour, milk, in fact everything has been thoroughly warmed before mixing. Mix the dough slowly with a wooden spoon and then knead as directed.

This amount will make two loaves, either twisted or in small bread pans. Bake forty-five minutes in a moderate oven.

If the bread is set in the morning use a cake of compressed yeast and bake the loaves in the afternoon.

INDIVIDUAL LOAVES

Make dough according to the above recipe. Work small pieces of dough into strands a finger long, and take three strands for each loaf. Make small as possible, brush with beaten egg; or sweetened water and sprinkle with poppy seed (mohn). Allow them to rise before setting them in the oven. These are called "Vienna loaves" and are used at weddings, parties and for the Succoth festival in the Succah.

If one-half cake of yeast has been used, the half cake of yeast which is left over, can be kept in good condition several days by rewrapping it in the tinfoil and keeping it in a cool, dry place.

BUTTERBARCHES

Dissolve one cake of compressed yeast in one-half cup of lukewarm milk, add a teaspoon of salt, and a tablespoon of sugar and let it rise. Then make a soft dough of eight cups of sifted flour and as much milk as is required to work it, about two cups; add the yeast, one-half cup of sugar, four tablespoons of butter dissolved in the warm milk, the grated peel of a lemon, two or three dozen raisins seeded, and two eggs well beaten. Work this dough perfectly smooth with the palm of your hand, adding more flour if necessary. It is hardly possible to tell the exact amount of flour to use; experience will teach you when you have added enough. Different brands of flour vary, some being drier than others. Work the dough as directed, set it aside covered until it is double the bulk of the original piece of dough. Then work again and divide the dough into two parts, and divide each of the pieces of dough into three parts. Work the six pieces of dough thoroughly and then roll each piece into a long strand; three of which are to be longer than the other three. Braid the three long strands into one braid (should be thicker in the centre than at the end), and braid the shorter strands into one braid and lay it on, top of the long braid, pressing the ends together. Butter a long baking-pan, lift the barches into the pan and set in a warm place to rise again for about one-half hour. Then brush the top with beaten egg and sprinkle poppy seed all over the top. Bake in a moderate oven one hour.

BARCHES

These are to be used for a meat meal and are made in the same manner as butter barches, omitting the milk and butter; use water and a little shortening of dripping or rendered fat or a vegetable oil; grate a dozen almonds (blanched) and add with two well-beaten eggs, one-half cup of sugar, salt, raisins and the grated peel of one lemon. Work just as you would butter barches. Bake one hour in moderate oven. Wrap in a damp, clean towel as soon as baked to prevent the crust from becoming too hard.

POTATO BREAD

Add one medium-sized mashed boiled potato to any of the foregoing recipes. This will give a more moist bread, which retains its freshness longer.

GRAHAM BREAD

Dissolve one cake of compressed yeast and four tablespoons of light brown sugar or molasses in one cup of lukewarm water and one cup of milk which has been scalded and cooled to lukewarm. Add two tablespoons of melted butter, then four cups of Graham flour and one cup of white flour (sifted), adding flour gradually, and one teaspoon of salt. Knead thoroughly, being sure to keep dough soft. Cover and set aside in a warm place to rise for about two hours. When double in bulk, turn out on kneading board, mold into loaves, and place in well-greased pans, cover and set to rise again —about one hour or until light. Bake one hour, in a slower oven than for white bread. If wanted for overnight use one-half cake of yeast and an extra half teaspoon of salt.

GLUTEN BREAD

Dissolve one cake of compressed yeast and one tablespoon of sugar in one cup of milk, scalded and cooled, and one cup of lukewarm water; add one level tablespoon of butter then three cups of gluten flour gradually, and one teaspoon of salt. Knead thoroughly until smooth and elastic; place in well-greased bowl; cover and set aside in a warm place, free from draught, to rise until light, which should be in about two hours. Mold into loaves; place in greased pans, filling them half full. Cover, let rise again, and when double in bulk, which should be in about one hour, bake in moderate oven forty-five minutes.

This will make two one-pound loaves. For diet use omit shortening and sugar.

RAISIN BREAD

Make dough as directed for Butterbarches, using one-quarter cup of raisins and omitting the lemon and egg. Form in loaves, fill well-greased pans half full; cover and let rise until light; about one hour. Glaze with egg diluted with water, and bake forty-five minutes.

ROLLED OATS BREAD

Pour two cups of boiling water over two cups of rolled oats, cover and let stand until lukewarm. Dissolve one cake of compressed yeast and one-fourth cup of brown sugar in one-half cup of lukewarm water, add two tablespoons of shortening, the oatmeal and the water in which it has been swelling. Beat well, add about three cups of flour to make a dough, also add one teaspoon of salt. Let rise until it doubles in bulk. Mold into two loaves in pan and bake forty-five minutes.

POTATO-RYE BREAD

Cook one quart of potatoes diced, in boiling water until tender. Strain, reserving potato water. Measure and add enough more water to make three cups. Let come to a boil, add one-quarter cup of salt, and very gradually one and one-quarter cups of cornmeal. Cook two minutes, stirring constantly until thick. Remove from fire, add two tablespoons of any kind of fat, the potatoes riced or mashed and when cooled two cups of flour; then one tablespoon of sugar and one cake of yeast dissolved in one cup of lukewarm water. Mix and knead to a stiff dough adding wheat flour to keep it from sticking. Cover, set aside in a warm place overnight, or until double its bulk. Shape into four loaves, let rise again; bake in a moderate oven one hour or more, until well done. Glaze with egg diluted with water before putting in the oven. These loaves will keep moist one week.

RYE BREAD (AMERICAN) No. 1

Dissolve one cake compressed yeast in two cups of lukewarm water and one cup of milk which has been scalded and cooled; or if so desired the milk may be omitted and all water used; add two and one-half cups of rye flour or enough to make a sponge. Beat well; cover and set aside in a warm place, free from draught, to rise about two hours. When light add one and one-half cups of sifted white flour, one tablespoon of melted butter or oil, two and one-half cups of rye flour to make a soft dough and last one tablespoon of salt. Turn on a board and knead or pound it five minutes. Place in greased bowl; cover and let rise until double in bulk—about two hours. Turn on board and shape into loaves; place in floured shallow pans; cover and let rise again until light—about one hour. Brush with white of egg and water, to glaze. With sharp knife cut lightly three strokes diagonally across top, and place in oven. Bake in slower oven than for white bread. Caraway seeds may be used if desired.

By adding one-half cup of sour dough, left from previous baking, an acid flavor is obtained, which is considered by many a great improvement. This should be added to the sponge.

RYE BREAD, No. 2

Sift three cups of rye flour, three cups of wheat flour and two teaspoons of salt in a bowl. Dissolve one-half cake of compressed yeast or any other yeast in two cups of lukewarm water. When the yeast is dissolved pour it into the flour and make into a dough. Lay it on a kneading board, and knead until smooth and elastic, put it back into the bowl, cover with a towel, and set aside overnight to rise. Next morning, lay the dough on a biscuit or kneading board again and knead well. Make into a loaf, put into a pan, and when well risen, moisten the top with a little cold water and bake in a moderate oven.

ZWIEBEL PLATZ

Take a piece of rye bread dough. After it has risen sufficiently roll out quite thin, butter a long cake pan and put in the rolled dough. Brush with melted butter; chop some onions very fine, strew thickly on top of cake, sprinkle with salt, put flakes of butter here and there. Another way is to chop up parsley and use in place of onions. Then called "Petersilien Platz."

VARIETY BREAD

Dissolve one cake of compressed yeast in two cups of lukewarm water or milk, add two teaspoons of salt, three cups of bread or wheat flour, one cup of cornmeal, one cup of rye flour and one-half cup of dark molasses, and mix very thoroughly. Let rise, shape into loaves, let rise again and bake in a moderate oven for forty-five minutes.

ROLLS

Take bread dough, when ready to shape into loaves and make a long even roll. Cut into small even pieces, and shape with thumb and fingers into round balls. Set close together in a shallow pan, let rise until double the bulk, and bake in a hot oven from ten to twenty minutes. If crusty rolls are desired, set apart in a shallow pan, bake well, and cool in draft.

TEA ROLLS

Scald one cup of milk and when lukewarm dissolve one cake of compressed yeast and add one and one-half cups of flour. Beat thoroughly, cover and allow to stand until light. Add one-quarter cup of sugar, one and one-half teaspoons of salt, two eggs, one-third cup of butter and enough flour to knead. Allow to rise again until light. Shape into round or small oblong finger rolls, and place in buttered pans close together, when light bake in hot oven.

CRESCENT ROLLS

Take bread or kitchen dough, and when well risen, toss on floured baking board, roll into a square sheet, one-quarter inch thick. Spread with melted butter, and cut into six-inch squares, then cut each square into two equal parts through opposite corners, thus forming two triangles. Roll over and over from the longest side to the opposite corner and then shape the rolls into half moons or crescents. Place in floured or greased pans, rather far apart; brush with beaten yolk to which a little cold water has been added and sprinkle tops of crescents or horns with poppy seed. Set in warm place to and, when double its bulk, bake in hot oven until brown and crusty.

BUNS

Make same as tea rolls. When well risen mold into small round buns; place in well-greased pans, one inch apart. Coyer set aside to rise until light —about one hour. Brush with egg diluted with water; bake twenty minutes, just before removing from the oven, brush with sugar moistened with a little water.

RAISIN OR CURRANT BUNS

Boil two large potatoes and strain the water into a pitcher, dissolve two-thirds cake of yeast in a cup. Put potatoes in a pan with a cup of sugar; large lump of butter, and teaspoon of salt. The heat of potatoes will melt the sugar and butter. Mash with large masher to a cream; pour in rest of potato water, add pint of flour and mix together. Then cover and set in a warm place all night. In the morning add more flour, mix quickly and put currants or raisins in as you turn the dough. This will keep them from settling in the bottom of the bread. Put in hot pans and bake in a hot oven. This makes a delicious holiday bread. Eat with butter, hot or cold.

BREAD STICKS

Take pieces of raised bread dough, roll three-eighths inch thick and four or five inches long. Place in floured pan, far apart, brush tops with beaten yolk and poppy seed. Let rise, bake in a hot oven until brown.

FRENCH ROLLS

Prepare the yeast as for bread and work just the same; add one-quarter cup of butter, one-quarter cup of sugar, one whole egg and one egg yolk beaten very light, flavor with mace or a few gratings of lemon peel; work until it leaves the hand perfectly clean, then form into rolls, let raise, brush with beaten egg, place rolls in pan close together and bake.

BUTTERED TOAST

Slice even slices of baker's bread, not too thin, put in biscuit pan on the top rack of a very hot oven, brown nicely on one side, then turn and brown on the other, spread with butter, and a little powdered sugar, if desired, and serve at once. Or put the slices on a long fork, hold before a red coal fire, without flame, toast on both sides and proceed as above.

MILK OR CREAM TOAST

Toast as many slices of stale light bread as desired a light brown. Heat milk or cream, allowing one-half cup for each slice, add small lump of butter. When just at the boiling point, pour over bread which has been placed in dish, sprinkle with sugar and cinnamon, cover, and serve immediately. Nice for invalids.

CINNAMON TOAST FOR TEA

Bread cut thin and browned, but not dried.

Butter the toast while very hot, thinly and evenly, and sprinkle over each piece some powdered cinnamon and sugar.

ARME RITTER

Beat two eggs slightly, add one-half teaspoon of salt and two-thirds cup of milk; dip six slices of stale bread in the mixture. Have a griddle hot and well buttered; brown the bread on each side. Serve hot with cinnamon and sugar or a sauce.

COFFEE CAKES (KUCHEN)

RENDERED BUTTER

Procure as much country or Western butter as desired, you may get several pounds of it when it is cheap during the summer; or any butter unfit for table use may be made sweet and good for cooking purposes and will last for months, if prepared in the following manner: Place the butter in a deep, iron kettle, filling only half full to prevent boiling over. Set it on the fire where it will simmer slowly for several hours. Watch carefully that it does not boil over. Do not stir it, but from time to time skim it. When perfectly clear, and all the salt and sediment has settled at the bottom, the butter is done. Set aside a few minutes, then strain into stone jars through a fine sieve, and when cold tie up tightly with paper and cloth. Keep in a cool, dry place.

COFFEE CAKE (KUCHEN) DOUGH

Soak one-half ounce of yeast in one-half cup of lukewarm milk; when dissolved put in a bowl, or round agate pan, and stir in one cup of sifted flour, one teaspoon of sugar and one-fourth teaspoon of salt, mix thoroughly, and put in a warm place (not hot) to rise, from one to two hours.

When well risen, cream well together one cup of sugar and three-fourths cup of butter, then add three eggs, five cups of sifted flour, one cup of milk and one teaspoon of salt, mix together until light, then stir in the risen yeast, and with a spoon work well for ten minutes, and set aside to rise again, five or six hours or all night. Dough should not be very stiff. When well risen it can be used for cinnamon cake, pies or pocket books. This recipe makes one large cinnamon cake, three pies, and about one dozen pocket books. If set at night use half the quantity of yeast.

KAFFEE KUCHEN (CINNAMON)

Butter long and broad cake-pans thoroughly, roll out enough dough to cover them, and let it rise about half an hour before baking, then brush it well with melted butter. Sprinkle sugar and cinnamon on top and some chopped almonds. Take a small lump of butter, a very little flour, some sugar and cinnamon and rub it between the hands until it is like lumps of almonds, then strew on top of cakes.

CINNAMON ROLLS OR SCHNECKEN

Take half the kitchen dough. Roll one-half inch thick and spread well with melted butter. Sprinkle generously with scraped maple, brown or granulated sugar and cinnamon, then roll. Cut the roll into equal parts about one inch thick, place close together endwise in a spider, generously buttered, spread with one-fourth inch layer of brown, or maple sugar. Let rise until light, and bake ten to twenty minutes in a hot oven, a golden brown. Invert the spider, remove rolls and serve caramel side up.

ABGERUEHRTER KUGELHOPF

Soak one-half ounce of yeast or one cake compressed yeast in a very little lukewarm milk; add a pinch of salt and one tablespoon of sugar, stir it up smooth and set back of the stove to rise. In the meantime rub a scant cup of butter and a scant cup of powdered sugar to a cream, add gradually the yolks of four eggs, one at a time and add also the grated peel of a lemon. Sift two cups of flour into a bowl, make a depression in the centre, pour in, the yeast, one cup of lukewarm milk, and make a light batter of this. Add the creamed butter and eggs and stir until it forms blisters and leaves the bowl clean. Take one-half cup of cleaned and seeded dark raisins and cut up some citron very fine. Dredge flour over them before adding, and if necessary, add more flour to the dough, which should be of the consistency of cup cake batter. Last add the stiffly-beaten whites of the eggs. Place in a well-greased long or round pan with tube in centre; let rise until double in bulk, and bake in moderate oven until browned and thoroughly done.

PLAIN BUNT OR NAPF KUCHEN

Take one cake compressed yeast, add a pinch of salt, one tablespoon of sugar, and about two tablespoons of lukewarm water. Stir the yeast until it is a smooth paste and set it in a warm place to rise. Sift two and one-half cups of flour (use the same size cup for measuring everything you are going to use in your cake), make a depression in the centre, stir in the yeast and a scant cup of lukewarm milk, make batter, and let it rise until you have prepared the following: Rub one-half cup of butter and three-fourths cup of powdered sugar to a cream, just as for cup cake, then add gradually one egg at a time, using three altogether, and stirring all the time in one direction. Work in the risen batter two or three spoons at a time between each egg. Grate in the peel of a lemon or an orange. Butter the bunt-form well (do this always before you begin to work). Blanched almonds may be set in the grooves of the cake-form after buttering it. Put in the dough, set it in a warm place and let it rise for an hour and a half or two hours. Bake in a moderate oven one full hour, covered at first.

CHOCOLATE COFFEE CAKE

Pour a bunt kitchen dough into long, well-buttered tins, and when baked remove from the oven and cover thickly with boiled chocolate icing.

POCKET BOOKS

Take as much of the coffee cake dough as you desire, lay it on a well-floured biscuit board and mix just enough more flour with it to enable you to roll it out without sticking to the board. Roll out about one-fourth inch thick and cut the dough in squares about as long as your finger.

Beat the yolk of one egg and two tablespoons of milk together; wet each square well with the mixture, lay one raisin in the centre (after the seed has been removed from it), sprinkle thickly with sugar and cinnamon mixed together, then put a small dab of butter on top. Catch the four corners of each square together, so that the inside is protected. Lay the pocket books, not too closely together, in a greased pan and set aside to rise. When well risen bake in a moderately hot oven until well baked and browned nicely.

BOLA

Make a good, rich bread dough. Let it rise overnight; next morning; mix with dough two eggs; one-half pound of butter well kneaded; stand by fire until well risen. When risen, roll out into thin sheets and sprinkle with chopped almonds, citron, cinnamon and plenty of brown sugar and lumps of butter all through; roll up like jelly-roll, cut in pieces a finger long, grease pan, stand pieces in centre, others around and let rise before baking. Watch it well while baking.

FRENCH COFFEE CAKE (SAVARIN)

Soak one cake of compressed yeast in a little lukewarm water or milk. Put the yeast in a cup, add two tablespoons of lukewarm water, a pinch of salt and one tablespoon of sugar, stir it up well with a spoon and set back of the stove to rise. Rub one-half cup of butter to a cream, add one-third cup of powdered sugar and stir constantly in one direction. Add the yolks of four eggs, one at a time, and the grated peel of a lemon. Sift two cups of flour into a bowl, make a depression in the centre of the flour, pour in the yeast and one cup of lukewarm milk. Stir and make a light batter of this. Add the creamed butter and eggs, stir until it forms blisters and leaves the bowl clean; one-half cup of dark raisins, one-half cup of pounded almonds and a little citron, cut up very fine, and last the stiff-beaten whites of the eggs. Fill your cake forms which have been well-greased, set in a warm place to rise until double in bulk, about forty-five minutes, and bake in a moderate oven forty-five minutes. Fill the centre with whipped cream and serve with rum sauce.

BABA A LA PARISIENNE

Prepare the yeast as above; cream a scant cup of butter with four tablespoons of sugar, the grated peel of a lemon, add five eggs, one at a time, stirring each egg a few minutes before you add the next. Have ready two cups of sifted flour and add two spoonfuls between each egg until all is used. Make a soft dough of the yeast, a scant cup of lukewarm milk, add two spoonfuls between each egg until all is used up, a pinch of salt, and one cup of flour. Let it rise for fifteen minutes. Now mix all well, rub the form with butter, and blanch one-half cup of almonds, cut into long strips and strew all over the form. Fill in the mixture or cake batter, let it rise two hours and bake very slowly.

MOHN (POPPY SEED) ROLEY POLEY

Roll out a piece of dough large enough to cover your whole baking-board, roll thin. Let it rise until you have prepared the filling; grind one cup of black poppy seed in a coffee-mill as tight as possible and clean it well, throw away the first bit you grind so as not to have the coffee taste; put it on to boil with one cup of milk, add two tablespoons of butter, one-half cup of seeded raisins, one-half cup of walnuts or almonds chopped up fine, two tablespoons of molasses or syrup, and a little citron cut up fine. When thick, set it away to cool, and if not sweet enough add more sugar and flavor with vanilla. When this mixture has cooled, spread on the dough which has risen by this time. Take up one corner and roll it up, into a long roll, like a jelly-roll, put in a greased pan and let it rise an hour, then spread butter on top and bake very slowly. Let it get quite brown, so as to bake through thoroughly. When cold cut up in slices, as many as you are going to use at one time only.

MOHN WACHTEL

Take coffee cake dough. Let the dough rise again; for an hour, spread with a poppy seed mixture, after cutting into squares, fold into triangles and pinch the edges together. Lay in well-buttered pans, about two inches apart, and let them rise again, spread with poppy seed filling. Take one-half pound of poppy seed (mohn) which have previously been soaked in milk and then ground, add one-quarter of a pound of sugar and the yolks of three eggs.

Stir this all together in one direction until quite thick and then stir in the beaten whites to which you must add two ounces of sifted flour and one-quarter of a pound of melted butter. Fill the tartlets and bake. The poppy seed filling in Mohn Roley Poley may be used in the Mohn Wachtel if so desired.

MOHNTORTS

Line a deep pie-plate with a thin sheet of kuchen dough, let it rise about half an hour, then fill with a poppy seed filling same as used with Mohn Wachtel. Fill the pie-plates and bake.

SMALL MOHN CAKES

Roll coffee cake dough out quite thin, spread with melted butter (a brush is best for this purpose). Let it rise a little while, then sprinkle well with one cup of sugar, add one-half pound of ground poppy seed moistened with one-half cup of water, cut into strips about an inch wide and four-inches long; roll and put in a well-buttered pan to rise, leaving enough space between each and brush, with butter. Bake in moderate oven at first, then increase the heat; bake slowly.

BERLINER PFANNKUCHEN (PURIM KRAPFEN)

Take one and one-half cups of flour, a pinch of salt sifted into a deep bowl, one cup of lukewarm milk and three-fourths cake of compressed yeast which has been, dissolved in a little warm water and sugar. Stir into a dough, cover with a towel and set away in a warm place to rise. When well risen, take one-half cup of butter, one cup of sugar, a little salt and rub to a cream. Add two eggs well beaten, stir all well and add the risen dough, one teaspoon of salt and work in gradually five cups of sifted flour and the grated peel of a lemon. Stir the dough till it blisters and leaves the dish perfectly clean at the sides. Let the dough rise slowly for about two hours (all yeast dough is better if it rises slowly). Take a large baking-board, flour well and roll out the dough on it as thin as a double thickness of pasteboard. When it is all rolled out, cut with a round cutter the size of a tumbler. When all the dough has been cut out, beat up an egg. Spread the beaten egg; on the edge of each cake (spread only a few at a time for they would get too dry if all were done at once). Then put one-half teaspoon of marmalade, jam or jelly on the cake. Put another cake on top of one already spread, having cut it with a cutter a little bit smaller than the one used in the first place. This makes them stick better and prevents the preserves coming out while cooking. Set all away on a floured board or pan about two inches apart.

Spread the top of each cake with melted butter and let them rise from one to two hours. When ready to fry, heat at least two pounds of rendered butter or any good vegetable oil in a deep iron kettle. Try the butter with a small piece of dough. If it rises immediately, put in the doughnuts. In putting them in, place the side that is up on the board down in the hot butter. Do not crowd them in the kettle as they require room to rise and spread. Cover them with a lid. In a few seconds uncover. If they are light brown, turn them over on the other side but do not cover them again. When done they will have a white stripe around the centre. Take them up with a perforated skimmer, lay on a large platter, sprinkle with pulverized sugar. If the butter gets too hot take from the fire a minute. These are best eaten fresh.

The doughnuts may be baked in moderately hot oven and when half done glazed with sugar and white of egg.

TOPFA DALKELN. CHEESE CAKES (HUNGARIAN)

Take one-half ounce of yeast, mix with a little scalded milk which has cooled to lukewarm, one-half cup of flour and put aside in a warm place to rise. Allow two cups of scalded milk to become lukewarm. Add one pound of flour (four cups sifted flour) to the risen sponge, then the two cups of milk, mix these very well, cover with a cloth and put aside in a warm place to rise. Take one pound of sweet pot cheese, a pinch of salt, three egg yolks, rind of one lemon, one-half cup of light colored raisins and sugar to taste; mix very well and add the beaten whites and mix thoroughly. When the dough is very well risen, place on a pastry board, roll out and spread with melted butter, fold these edges over to the middle, then the top and bottom over, roll again and spread with butter, fold all sides in once more, roll, spread with butter, repeat the folding, roll out to one-half inch thickness, cut in three-inch squares, place a tablespoon of the cheese mixture in the centre of each square, fold over opposite corners, spread egg white over the top of each pocket, let rise fifteen minutes or one-half hour and bake in a hot oven; when they are well risen, lower heat and bake to a golden brown. This will make about thirty cakes. The dough in the above may be used with the following filling:

Boil and stone one-half pound of prunes, mash to a pulp, sweeten, add the grated peel of a lemon, some cinnamon, etc., and put one teaspoon of this into each square. Take up the corners, fasten them firmly, also pinch all along the edges and lay in a buttered pan, let them rise half an hour before baking. Spread them with melted butter, and bake a nice brown.

PUFFS (PURIM)

Make the dough same as for Berliner Pfannkuchen, and when well risen roll out on a floured board one-half inch thick, cut in triangles, lay on floured dishes or board to rise. When well risen, drop into a deep kettle of boiling butter and with a spoon baste with the butter until brown; remove with a perforated skimmer and sprinkle with powdered sugar.

KINDLECH

Into a large bowl sift one pound of fine flour. Make a depression in the centre and pour into it one yeast cake dissolved in a little milk. Let this remain until the milk and yeast have risen a little. Stir in the surrounding flour together with three well-beaten eggs, a quarter of a pound of butter, six ounces of sugar, a pinch of salt and two cups of lukewarm milk. Knead the whole into a smooth dough.

Roll this out very lightly on a well-floured board, brush over with a feather dipped in melted butter and strew thickly with chopped almonds, sultanas and currants. Next fold over about three fingers' width of the dough. Brush the upper surface of this fold with melted butter and strew with mixed fruit and almonds. Fold over again and repeat the operation until the whole of the dough is folded up in layer somewhat resembling a flattened, roley poley pudding. Brush the top well with another feather dipped in beaten egg and cut the whole into thick slices or fingers. Let them stand for half an hour and then bake for an hour in a rather slow oven.

A CHEAP COFFEE CAKE

This German coffee cake is made by kneading into a pint of bread dough one well-beaten egg, one-half cup of sugar, and a generous tablespoon of butter. The mixture is rolled flat, placed in a shallow pan, let rise again until very light, sprinkled with finely chopped nuts, dusted over with sugar and cinnamon and baked in a quick oven.

BOHEMIAN KOLATCHEN

Make kuchen dough. Add a little cinnamon and mace and one teaspoon of anise seed, well pounded, or flavor to taste. Let rise till very light, then take out on mixing board and roll out to about one-half inch in thickness. Cut in rounds three inches in diameter and lay on a well-buttered pan, pressing down the centre of each so as to raise a ridge around the edge. When well risen, brush the top over with stiffly-beaten white of an egg and sprinkle with granulated sugar.

ZWIEBACK

Scald one-half cup of milk and when lukewarm add to one cake of compressed yeast. Add one-fourth cup of sugar, one-fourth cup of melted butter, one-half teaspoon of salt and three eggs unbeaten, one-half teaspoon of powdered anise and enough flour to handle. Let rise until light. Make into oblong rolls the length of middle finger and place together in a buttered pan in parallel rows, two inches apart. Let rise again and bake twenty minutes. When cold, cut in one-half inch slices and brown evenly in the oven.

SOUR CREAM KOLATCHEN

Cream one-half cup of butter, add five yolks, two tablespoons of sugar, grated rind of a lemon, one cup of thick sour cream and one ounce or two cakes of yeast dissolved with a little sugar in two tablespoons of lukewarm milk. Stir all together and add three cups of flour; mix and drop from end of teaspoon on well-greased pans. Let rise until light in a warm place. Place a raisin or cherry on the top of each cake, spread with beaten white of egg, sprinkle with sugar and bake ten minutes in a hot oven.

RUSSIAN TEA CAKES

Mix one cup of sugar, one cup of eggs (about five), and one cup of sour cream with enough flour to roll. Toss on board, roll out one-fourth inch thick, spread with a thin layer of butter, fold the dough over, roll and spread again; repeat three or four times, using altogether three-fourths pound of brick butter. Then place dough in a bowl, cover, and let stand on ice to harden. Then roll as thin as possible, strew with one cup of chopped almonds, sugar and cinnamon, and cut into seven-inch strips. Roll each strip separately into a roll, cut into squares and strew top with chopped almonds, sugar and cinnamon. Bake in a hot oven.

WIENER KIPFEL

Dissolve one ounce of yeast in one-half cup of lukewarm milk, a pinch of salt and one tablespoon of sugar, set away in a warm place to rise. Sift one pound of flour into a deep bowl and make a dough of one cup of lukewarm milk and the yeast. Set it away until you have prepared the following: Rub a quarter of a pound of butter and four ounces of sugar to a cream, adding yolks of three eggs and one whole egg. Add this to the dough and work well. Let it rise about one hour, then roll out on a well-floured board, just as you would for cookies and let it rise again for at least one-half hour. Spread with beaten whites of eggs, raisins, almonds and citron. Cut dough into triangles. Pinch the edges together. Lay them in well-buttered pans about two inches apart and let then rise again. Then spread again with stiff-beaten whites of eggs and lay a few pounded almonds on each one. Bake a light yellow.

SPICE ROLL

Roll out coffee cake dough quite thin and let it rise half an hour, brush with melted butter and make a filling of the following: Grate some lebkuchen or plain gingerbread; add one-half cup of almonds or nuts, one cup of seeded raisins and one cup of cleaned currants. Strew these all over the dough together with some brown sugar and a little syrup. Spice with cinnamon and roll. Spread with butter and let it rise for an hour. Bake brown.

WIENER STUDENTEN KIPFEL

Make dough same as for Wiener Kipfel. Roll it out quite thin on a well-floured board and let it rise. Cut also into triangles (before you cut them, spread with melted butter). Mix one cup of chopped fresh walnuts with one cup of brown sugar, juice of a lemon, or grind the nuts; add cream to make a paste, sugar to taste and flavor with vanilla, and fill the triangles with the mixture. Take up the three corners and pinch together tightly. Set in well-buttered pans and let them rise again and spread or brush each one with melted butter. Bake a light brown.

YEAST KRANTZ

Take coffee cake dough, add one-fourth cup of washed currants. Let rise in warm place, then toss on floured board. Divide into three or four equal parts, roll each part into a long strand and work the strands together to form one large braid. Place braid in form of a circle in greased baking-pan or twist the braid to resemble the figure eight, pretzel shape. Let rise again in a warm place and bake in a moderate oven one-half hour or until thoroughly done. Brush with beaten eggs and sugar, sprinkle with a few chopped almonds. Return to oven to brown slightly.

STOLLEN

Sift two pounds of flour into a bowl and set a sponge in it with one cake of compressed yeast, one teaspoon of salt, one pint of lukewarm milk and one tablespoon of sugar. When this has risen, add one-half pound of creamed butter, a quarter of a pound of seeded raisins and one-quarter of a pound of sugar, yolks of four eggs, four ounces of powdered almonds, and the grated peel of a lemon. Work all well, beating with the hands, not kneading. Let this dough rise at least three hours, roll, press down the centre and fold over double, then form into one or two long loaves, narrow at the end. Brush the top with melted butter, let rise again and bake three-quarters of an hour in a moderate oven.

APPLE CAKE (KUCHEN)

After the pan is greased with butter, roll out a piece of dough quite thin, lay it in the pan, press a rim out of the dough all around the pan and let it rise for about ten minutes. Pare five large apples, core and quarter them, dipping each piece in melted butter before laying on the cake, sprinkle bountifully with sugar (brown being preferable to white for this purpose) and cinnamon. See that you have tart apples. Leave the cake in the pans and cut out the pieces just as you would want to serve them. If they stick to the pan, set the pan on top of the hot stove for a minute and the cake will then come out.

CHEESE CAKE OR PIE

Take one and one-half cups of cheese, rub smooth with a silver or wooden spoon through a colander or sieve, then rub a piece of sweet butter the size of an egg to a cream, add gradually one-half cup of sugar and the yolks of three eggs, a pinch of salt, grate in the peel of a lemon, one-half cup of cleaned currants and a little citron cut up very fine. Line two pie-plates with some kuchen dough or pie dough (See "Coffee Cakes (Kuchen)"), roll it out quite thin, butter the pie-plates quite heavily, and let the dough in them rise at least a quarter of an hour before putting in the cheese mixture, for it must be baked immediately after the cheese is put in, and just before you put the cheese into the plates whip up the whites of the eggs to a very stiff froth and stir through the cheese mixture.

CHERRY CAKE

Line a cake-pan, which has been well-buttered, with a thin layer of kuchen dough. Stone two pounds of cherries and lay them on a sieve with a dish underneath to catch the juice. Sprinkle sugar over them and bake. In the meantime beat up four eggs with a cup of sugar, beat until light and add the cherry juice. Draw the kuchen to the oven door, pour this mixture over it and bake.

PEACH KUCHEN

Grease your cake-pans thoroughly with good clarified butter, then line them with a rich coffee cake dough which has been rolled very thin and set in a warm place to rise. Then pare and quarter enough peaches to cover the dough. Lay the peaches in rows and sweeten and set in oven to bake. Make a meringue quickly as possible and pour over the cakes and bake a light brown.

FRESH PRUNE CAKE (KUCHEN)

Line a greased biscuit-pan with some of the coffee cake dough. Roll the dough thin and let it come up on the sides of the pan, then set aside to rise. When risen, cut the prunes in halves (they must be the fresh ones, not dried), lay in rows thickly and close together all over the bottom of the pan, do not leave any space between the prunes. Sprinkle very thickly with sugar, lightly with cinnamon, and lay bits of fresh butter all over the top. Bake until done in a moderately hot oven.

PRUNE CAKE (KUCHEN)

Line one or two plates with a thin roll of kuchen dough and let it rise again in the pans which have been heavily greased. Have some prunes boiled very soft, take out the kernels, mash them until like mush, sweeten to taste, add cinnamon and grated peel of a lemon or lemon juice, put in the lined pie-plates and bake immediately. Serve with whipped cream, sweetened and flavored.

HUCKLEBERRY KUCHEN

Line your cake-pans, which should be long and narrow, with a rich kuchen dough, having previously greased them well. Make a paste of cornstarch, one cup of milk, one tablespoon of butter and one teaspoon of cornstarch wet with cold milk. Boil until thick, sweeten and flavor with vanilla and spread on top of the cake dough, then sprinkle thickly with huckleberries which have been carefully picked, sugared and sprinkled with ground cinnamon. Bake in a quick oven.

HUCKLEBERRY PIE

Clean, pick and wash two cups of huckleberries, then drain them. Beat yolk of one egg and two tablespoons of sugar until light, add one tablespoon of milk, then the drained berries. Line one pie-plate with rich pastry or cookie dough, pour on it the berry mixture, put in the oven and bake light brown; remove from the oven, spread with a meringue made of the white of the egg beaten stiff, and two tablespoons of sugar added. Brown nicely. The white can be beaten with the yolk and sugar, if preferred.

MUFFINS AND BISCUITS

BAKING-POWDER

Put eight ounces of bicarbonate of soda, one ounce of tartaric acid and one package of high-grade cornstarch together and sift them thoroughly five times. Keep closely covered in glass jars or tin boxes.

BAKING-POWDER BATTERS

Batter is a mixture of flour with sufficient liquid to make it thin enough to be beaten.

Pour-batter requires one measure of liquid to one measure of flour.

Drop-batter requires one measure of liquid to two measures of flour.

To make a batter. Sift flour before measuring. Put flour by spoonfuls into the cup; do not press or shake down. Mix and sift dry ingredients. Measure dry, then liquid ingredients, shortening may be rubbed or chopped in while cold, or creamed; or it may be melted and then added to dry ingredients, or added after the liquid. Use two teaspoons of baking-powder to one cup of flour. If eggs are used, less baking-powder will be required.

When sour milk is used, take one level teaspoon of soda to a pint of milk; when molasses is used, take one teaspoon of soda or baking-powder to each cup of molasses.

Mix dry materials in one bowl and liquids in another, combine them quickly, handle as little as possible and put at once into the oven.

The oven for baking biscuits should be hot enough to brown a teaspoon of flour in one minute.

BROWN BREAD

Mix and sift together one cup each of rye, graham flour, corn-meal and one teaspoon of salt. Dissolve one teaspoon of soda in one cup of molasses. Add alternately to flour with two cups of sour milk. Grease one-pound baking-powder cans, put in the dough and boil two and one-half hours, keeping the water always three-fourths up around the tins. Turn out on baking-tins and place in the oven fifteen minutes to brown.

To be eaten warm, whatever is left over can be steamed again or toasted.

CORN BREAD

Mix and sift one cup of corn-meal, one cup of flour, two tablespoons of sugar, one-half teaspoon of salt, three teaspoons of baking-powder. Melt one tablespoon of butter and add to one egg; mix milk and egg and beat this into the dry ingredients, pour this mixture into well-greased tins and bake in a hot oven one-half hour. Cut in squares and serve hot. Bake in gem tins if preferred.

BRAN BREAD

Sift four teaspoons of soda, two teaspoons of salt with four cups of white flour, add four cups of bran flour and mix well. Add one cup of molasses and four cups of sweet milk. Use chopped nuts or raisins or both as desired. This will make three or four flat loaves. Place in greased pans (four and a half by nine inches), and bake one hour in a moderate oven.

JOHNNIE CAKE

Mix one cup flour and two cups corn-meal, one heaping teaspoon of soda, one-half cup sugar, add two eggs beaten with one and one-half cups of buttermilk, one half cup of molasses and one-half cup of shortening, melted. Beat all ingredients as fast as possible for a minute. Pour the dough into a warm, well-buttered pan and bake quickly and steadily for half an hour. The dough should be as soft as gingerbread dough. Serve hot.

EGGLESS GINGERBREAD WITH CHEESE

Sift two cups of flour, one teaspoon of soda, one-half teaspoon of salt and two teaspoons of ginger. Melt three-fourths cup of grated cheese in one-half cup of hot water, add one-half cup of molasses and blend perfectly. Add the flour and seasonings very gradually and beat thoroughly. Bake in muffin rings for fifteen minutes and serve while warm.

GINGERBREAD

To one cup of molasses add one cup of milk, sour or sweet, dissolve one teaspoon of soda in the milk, one tablespoon of butter, one or two eggs, one teaspoon of ginger and one of ground cinnamon, add enough sifted flour to make a light batter. Bake in a shallow pan.

WHITE NUT BREAD

Mix two and one-half cups of flour, four teaspoons of baking-powder, one-half teaspoon of salt, one-half cup of sugar and one-half cup of walnut meats, broken; add one egg beaten with one cup of milk and let this mixture stand for about twenty minutes in well-greased breadpan before placing in a moderate oven to bake. Bake about an hour. Better day after it is made.

BAKING-POWDER BISCUITS

Sift two cups of flour with one-half teaspoon of salt, four teaspoons of baking-powder, and four tablespoons of butter; cut butter in with two knives and mix with one-half to two-thirds cup of water or milk, stir this in quickly with a knife, when well mixed place on a well-floured board and roll out about one inch thick, work quickly, cut with a biscuit cutter or the cover of a half-pound baking-powder can; place on a greased pan and bake quickly in a well-heated quick oven tea to fifteen minutes.

Butter substitutes may be used in place of butter.

DROP BISCUIT

Add to ingredients for baking-powder biscuit enough more milk or water to make a thick drop batter, about two tablespoons; mix as directed for biscuit, drop by spoonfuls an inch apart on a greased baking-sheet or into greased gem pans, small size.

The more crust the more palatable these biscuits are. The mixture should not be soft enough to run. Bake in a hot oven ten to twelve minutes.

SOUR MILK BISCUITS

Mix and sift two cups of flour, one-half teaspoon of salt and one-half teaspoon of soda; cut in one tablespoon of butter, stir in with a knife enough sour milk to make a soft dough. Roll one-half inch thick; cut in small rounds and bake in a quick oven about twenty minutes.

MUFFINS.

Light the burners of the gas oven before beginning to mix the muffins and work rapidly. Place in a mixing-bowl one well-beaten egg, two tablespoons of butter, one tablespoon of sugar, one-half teaspoon of salt, one scant cup of milk and two teaspoons of baking-powder that have been sifted with sufficient flour to form a batter that will "ribbon" from the spoon. Beat the batter steadily for five minutes, stir in one tablespoon of melted butter and bake in muffin-pans in a quick oven. These muffins will bake in ten minutes if pans are only half filled.

BRAN MUFFINS

Sift one-half cup of white flour with one teaspoon of soda; mix three tablespoons of molasses with one tablespoon of butter, add two cups of bran, one and one-half cups of sweet milk, then add the flour and one-half teaspoon of salt, stir all together; one-half cup of chopped dates or raisins may be added if so desired. Bake in muffin-pans in a moderate oven thirty minutes.

CORN MUFFINS, No. 1

Beat the yolks and whites of two eggs separately. Add to this two cups of flour, of which one is a full cup of white and three-quarters of the corn-meal. This must be sifted three times. Put into this flour two teaspoons of baking-powder, together with a pinch of salt. Mix the prepared flour with a little boiling water, adding the eggs; also a little sugar may be put in, if desired. Then add enough tepid milk to make the mixture into a batter, after which pour into your pans; or, if corn-bread is desired, into the plain pan (thin). Bake in a quick oven. This quantity makes a dozen muffins. Butter your pan well, or the small gem-pans, according to which is used, and in so doing heat the pan a little.

CORN MUFFINS, No. 2

Mix one cup of white flour; one-half cup of corn-meal, one tablespoon of sugar, one-half teaspoon of salt and one-half teaspoon of soda, add one egg beaten into one cup of sour milk and one tablespoon of melted butter. Beat thoroughly and bake in well-greased tins.

GRAHAM MUFFINS

Mix one cup of Graham flour, one cup of wheat flour, one-half teaspoon of salt, two teaspoons of baking-powder, add to this one tablespoon of melted butter creamed with one-half cup of sugar and one well-beaten egg, moisten with one and one-half cups of milk. Beat all well and bake in muffin-tins in moderately hot oven one-half hour.

WHEAT MUFFINS

Mix two cups of flour, one-half teaspoon of salt, three teaspoons of baking-powder, two tablespoons of sugar and sift these ingredients twice, rub in one tablespoon of butter. Separate one egg. Beat the yolk and add it to one cup of milk and one teaspoon of molasses. Mix with the dry ingredients and stir until smooth. Fold in the beaten white of egg and pour into hot, well-greased muffin-tins. Bake fifteen to twenty minutes in hot oven.

RICE MUFFINS

Beat one cup of cold rice, two eggs, one cup of sweet milk, one teaspoon of salt, one tablespoon of sugar, two teaspoons of baking-powder, enough flour to make a stiff batter and lastly one tablespoon of melted butter. Bake in muffin-tins.

RYE FLOUR MUFFINS

Sift one and one-half cups of rye flour with one-half teaspoon of salt and one teaspoon of baking soda; add one-half cup of molasses and one well-beaten egg or one-half cup of water if the egg is omitted, one-quarter cup of chopped raisins and four tablespoons of melted shortening—butter, or any good butter substitute will do. Bake in muffin-pans in rather hot oven twenty-five minutes. Fill pans three-fourths full.

GLUTEN GEMS

Beat the yolks of two eggs, add one cup of milk; then one and one-half cups of gluten flour, two teaspoons of baking powder; beat well, stir in the whites of the two eggs, and bake in hot buttered gem pans about twenty minutes.

EGGLESS GINGER GEMS

Mix one-half cup of molasses, one-half cup of sugar, one tablespoon of butter, and warm slightly; beat up well and stir at least ten minutes. Add the following spices: one-half teaspoon each of ginger and cinnamon; and gradually one-half cup of milk and two and one-half cups of sifted flour in which has been sifted two teaspoons of baking powder. One-fourth cup of currants or seeded raisins may be added. Bake in well-greased gem pans and eat warm for tea or lunch.

POPOVERS

Mix to a smooth batter two cups each of milk and well-sifted flour, the yolks of three fresh eggs and a teaspoon of salt. Butter well the inside of six or eight deep earthen popover cups and stand them in a pan in a hot oven. While the cups are heating, beat to a froth the whites of the three eggs and stir them quickly in the batter. Open the oven door, pull the pan forward, pour the batter in the hot buttered cups up to the brim. Push the pan back, close the oven door, and bake the popovers till they rise well and are brown at the sides where they part from the clips. Serve them hot, folded lightly in a napkin.

ONE-EGG WAFFLES

Mix one and one-half cups of flour, one teaspoon of baking powder, one-quarter teaspoon of salt; add one and three-fourths cups of milk, add the milk slowly; then one well-beaten egg and two tablespoons of melted butter; drop by spoonfuls on a hot buttered waffle iron, putting one tablespoon in each section of the iron. Bake and turn, browning both sides carefully; remove from the iron; pile one on top of the other and serve at once.

THREE-EGG WAFFLES

Mix two cups of flour, one teaspoon of baking-powder, one half teaspoon of salt, and sift these ingredients; add the yolks of three eggs beaten and stirred into one and one-fourth cups of milk; then add one tablespoon of melted butter and fold in the whites of the eggs. Bake and serve as directed under One-Egg Waffles.

DOUGHNUTS

Mix two and one-half tablespoons of melted butter, one cup of granulated sugar, two eggs, one cup of milk, one-half nutmeg grated, sifted flour enough to make a batter as stiff as biscuit dough; add two teaspoons of baking-powder and one teaspoon of salt to the sifted flour. Flour your board well, roll dough out about half an inch thick, and cut into pieces three inches long and one inch wide. Cut a slit about an inch long in the centre of each strip and pull one end through this slit. Fry quickly in hot Crisco. Sprinkle powdered sugar on top of each doughnut.

FRENCH DOUGHNUTS

French doughnuts are much daintier than the ordinary ones, and are easily made. Take one-half pint of water, one-half pint of milk, six ounces of butter, one-half pound of flour, and six eggs. Heat the butter, milk, and water, and when it boils remove from the fire and stir in the flour, using a wooden spoon. When well mixed, stir in the eggs, whipping each one in separately until you have a hard batter. Now pour your dough into a pastry bag. This is an ordinary cheesecloth bag, one corner of which has a tiny tin funnel, with a fluted or fancy edge. (These little tins may be purchased at any tinware store.) It should be very small, not over two inches high at the most, so the dough may be easily squeezed through it. Pour the paste on buttered paper, making into ring shapes. Fry in hot oil or butter substitute. Dust with powdered sugar.

CRULLERS

Cream two tablespoons of butter with one-half cup of sugar, then beat in one at a time two whole eggs. Mix well, then add one-half cup of milk, two teaspoons of baking-powder, and sufficient flour to make a soft batter to roll out. (Try three cupfuls and then add as much more flour as necessary.) Last, add one-half teaspoon cinnamon. Roll one-half inch thick, cut in strips one inch wide, three inches long and fry in hot Crisco.

STRAWBERRY SHORTCAKE (BISCUIT DOUGH)

Mix two cups of flour, four teaspoons of baking-powder, one-half teaspoon of salt, one tablespoon of sugar; work one-quarter cup of butter with tips of fingers, and add three-quarters of a cup of milk gradually. Toss on floured board, divide in two parts. Pat, roll out and bake twelve minutes in hot oven in layer-cake tins. Split and spread with butter. Pick, hull, and drain berries. Sweeten one to one and one-half boxes of strawberries to taste. Crush slightly and put between and on top of short cake. Allow from one to one and one-half boxes of berries to each short cake. Serve with cream, plain or whipped.

Strawberries make the best short cake, but other berries and sliced peaches are also good.

DOUGH FOR OPEN FACE PIES

The directions for making the dough for Cinnamon Buns may be followed in making the under crust for fruit pies, such as apple, plum, huckleberry and peach.

Enough for two pies. Drippings and water may be substituted for butter and milk respectively.

CINNAMON BUNS

Sift together one pint of flour, one tablespoon of sugar, one-half teaspoon of salt, two teaspoons of baking-powder. Rub in two tablespoons of butter, mix with milk to soft dough. Roll out one-half inch thick, spread with soft butter, granulated sugar, and powdered cinnamon. Roll up like jelly roll, cut in inch slices, lay close together in greased pan, and bake in quick oven.

FRUIT WHEELS

Sift together two cups of flour, two teaspoons of baking-powder, one-half teaspoon of salt, one tablespoon of sugar. Rub in two large tablespoons of butter. Mix to soft dough with milk; roll out one-half inch thick. Spread thickly with soft butter, dust with one teaspoon of flour, four tablespoons of granulated sugar, one teaspoon of cinnamon; sprinkle over one-half cup each of seeded and cut raisins, chopped citron, and cleaned currants. Roll up, cut in one-inch slices, put one inch apart on greased, flat pans, and bake in hot oven.

PANCAKES, FRITTERS, Etc.

BUCKWHEAT CAKES
Dissolve one cake of compressed yeast and two level teaspoons of brown sugar in two cups of lukewarm water and one cup of milk, scalded and cooled; add two cups of buckwheat and one cup of sifted white flour gradually and one and one-half teaspoons of salt. Beat until smooth; cover and set aside in a warm place, free from draft, to rise about one hour. When light stir well and bake on a hot griddle. If wanted for overnight, use only one-fourth cake of yeast and an extra half teaspoon of salt. Cover and keep in a cool place.

GERMAN PANCAKES, No. 1
Beat two eggs very thoroughly without separating the yolks and whites; add one-half teaspoon of salt, sift in two and one-half tablespoons of flour, add one cup of milk gradually at first, and beat the whole very well. Melt one tablespoon of butter in a large frying-pan, turn mixture in and cook slowly until brown underneath. Grease the bottom of a large pie plate, slip the pancake on the plate; add the other tablespoon of butter to the frying-pan; when hot, turn uncooked side of pancake down and brown. Serve at once with sugar and lemon slices or with any desired preserve or syrup. This pancake may be served rolled like a jelly roll.

GERMAN PANCAKES, No. 2
Beat two eggs until very light, add one-half cup of flour and one-half teaspoon of salt and beat again; then add one cup of milk slowly, and beat thoroughly. Heat a generous quantity of butter in a frying-pan and pour all the batter into this at one time; place on a hot stove for one minute; then remove to a brisk oven; the edges will turn up on sides of pan in a few minutes; then reduce heat and cook more slowly until light, crisp and brown, about seven minutes. Take it out, slide it carefully on a hot plate, sprinkle plentifully with powdered sugar and send to the table with six lemon slices.

GERMAN PANCAKES, No. 3
Beat the yolks of four eggs until very light, then add one-half cup of milk and stir in three-quarters cup of sifted flour, one-eighth teaspoon of

baking-powder, a pinch of salt, and lastly, just before frying, add the stiffly-beaten whites of eggs and mix well together. Put on fire an iron skillet with a close-fitting top; heat in two tablespoons of rendered butter; when very hot, pour in enough of the batter to cover the bottom of the skillet, cover at once with the top, and when the pancake is brown on one side, remove the top and let it brown on the other side. Take it up with a perforated skimmer, lay on a plate and sprinkle with powdered sugar and some lemon juice. Serve at once. Pancakes must only be made and fried when ready to be eaten, as they fall from standing.

BREAD PANCAKES

Soak stale bread overnight in sour milk, mash the bread fine in the morning, and put in one-half teaspoon of salt, two eggs, two teaspoons of baking soda, dissolved in hot water, and thicken with finely sifted flour.

RICE PANCAKES OR GRIDDLE CAKES

Boil in a double boiler one pint of milk, three tablespoons of rice and two tablespoons of granulated sugar. It will take from fifty to sixty minutes for the rice to be thoroughly cooked, and the mixture to thicken. Remove from the fire and when a little cool, add one tablespoon of vanilla and the yolk of egg into which one tablespoon of flour has been smoothly stirred. Mix all thoroughly together, then pour, by spoonfuls, on hot buttered griddle. Let the cakes brown on one side, and turn over, and brown on the other.

GRIMSLICH

Half a loaf of bread, which has been soaked and pressed, two eggs; one-half cup of sugar, one-fourth cup raisins, one tablespoon of cinnamon, and one-fourth cup of almonds pounded fine. Beat whites to a froth and add last. Drop by tablespoonful and fry. Serve with stewed fruit. Pieces of stale bread can be used. Soak in tepid water. Squeeze water thoroughly from bread and make as directed.

POTATO PANCAKES

Peel six large potatoes and soak several hours in cold water; grate, drain, and for every pint allow two eggs, about one tablespoon of flour, one-half teaspoon of salt, a little pepper; a little onion juice may be added if so desired. Beat eggs well and mix with the rest of the ingredients. Drop by spoonfuls on a hot greased spider in small cakes. Turn and brown on both sides. Serve with apple sauce.

When eggs are very expensive the cakes can be made with one egg.

When required for a meat meal, the pancakes may be fried in drippings; the edges will be much more crisp than when fried in butter, which burns so readily.

POTATO CAKES

Made just as pancakes, only baked in the oven in a long cake pan with plenty of butter or drippings under and above.

SOUR MILK PANCAKES

Mash fine and dissolve one level teaspoon of baking-soda in three cups of sour milk; beat one egg well; then put in a little salt and one-half cup of flour; stir in the milk, make a smooth batter, and last stir in one tablespoon of syrup. Bake on a hot griddle.

FRENCH PANCAKE

Stir three egg-yolks with one-half teaspoon of salt and one-quarter cup of flour, until smooth; add one cup of cold milk gradually, then fold in the beaten whites. Heat pan, add two tablespoons of butter and when hot pour in pancake; let cook slowly and evenly on one side, finish baking in oven.

CHEESE BLINTZES

With a fork beat up one egg, one-half teaspoon of salt, add one cup of water and one cup of sifted flour, beat until smooth. Grease a frying-pan very slightly with butter or oil, pour in two tablespoons of the batter, tilting the pan so as to allow the batter to run all over the pan. Fry over a low heat on one side only, turn out the semi-cooked cakes on a clean cloth with the uncooked side uppermost; let cool. Prepare a filling as for cheese kreplich, using one-half pound of potcheese, a piece of butter size of an egg, add one egg, pinch of salt, a little cinnamon and sugar to taste and grated peel of a lemon. Spread this mixture on the cooled dough, fold over and tuck the edges in well. Then sprinkle with powdered sugar and cinnamon, and fry in plenty of oil or butter. These blintzes are served hot.

SWEET BLINTZES

These little pancakes may be filled with the fruit filling in following recipe; or with a poppy seed filling using one cup of seed and adding one cup of sugar, moistening with one-half cup of water. The recipe given for the dough makes only six blintzes and where more are required double or triple the quantities given to make amount desired.

For Purim, fold blintzes in triangular shapes. Fry as directed.

BLINTZES

Make dough as directed for cheese blintzes. Filling may be made of force meat, highly seasoned; fry in hot fat, or filling may be made of one-half pound of apples, peeled and cored and then minced with one ounce of ground sweet almonds, one ounce of powdered sugar, a pinch of cinnamon, juice of one-half lemon; mix well and bind with the beaten white of egg.

Spread either of these mixtures on the dough, fold over and tuck edges in well. Fry in plenty of oil or fat.

Sprinkle those containing the fruit mixture with sugar and cinnamon. These may be served either hot or cold.

FRITTER BATTER

Mix and sift one and one-third cups of flour, two teaspoons of baking-powder, one-quarter teaspoon of salt, and add two-thirds cup of milk or water gradually, and one egg; well beaten. For fruit batter add a little sugar, for vegetables pepper and salt.

BELL FRITTERS

Stir three eggs until very light, then stir in one cup of sweet milk, then sift in three cups sifted flour; beat for ten minutes, then add three teaspoons of baking-powder and fry by spoonfuls in hot oil. One-half this amount will be sufficient for three persons.

Serve with any sweet sauce.

APPLE FRITTERS

Choose four sour apples; pare, core and cut them into small slices. Stir into fritter batter and fry in boiling hot fat or oil. Drain on paper; sprinkle with powdered sugar and serve.

PINEAPPLE FRITTERS

Soak slices of pineapple in sherry or white wine with a little sugar and let stand one hour. Drain and dip slices in batter and fry in hot oil. Drain on brown paper and sprinkle with powdered sugar.

Fresh pears, apricots and peach fritters made the same as pineapple fritters. Bananas are cut in slices or mashed and added to batter.

ORANGE FRITTERS

Yolks of two eggs beaten with two spoons of sugar, stir into this the juice of quarter of a lemon and just enough flour to thicken like a batter; add the beaten whites and dip in one slice of orange at a time, take up with a large kitchen spoon and lay in the hot oil or butter-substitute and fry a nice brown. Sprinkle pulverized sugar on top.

MATRIMONIES

Sift three cups of flour in a bowl, pour in two scant cups of sour milk, beat very thoroughly, add one teaspoon of salt, the well-beaten yolks of three eggs, mix well, then add the stiffly-beaten whites of the eggs and one level teaspoon of soda sifted with one teaspoon of flour. Mix well and fry at once in very hot butter or butter-substitute. Baste the grease over them with a spoon until they are nicely browned. Serve with preserves.

QUEEN FRITTERS

Put in a deep skillet on the fire one cup of water, one-fourth cup of fresh butter; when it comes to a boil, stir in one cup of sifted flour and continue stirring until the dough leaves the side of the skillet clean. Remove from the fire and when cool break in three eggs, one at a time, stirring continually. Add a little salt. Mix all well, then drop pieces about the size of a walnut into plenty of boiling butter or Crisco and fry a light brown. Drain, make an opening in each, fill with preserves and sprinkle with sugar; serve at once.

VEGETABLE FRITTERS

Cook the vegetables thoroughly; drain them, chop fine and add to the batter. Drop in boiling hot fat, drain and dry on paper.

CORN FRITTERS

Grate two cups of corn from the cob. Ears that are too old for eating in the ordinary method will serve very well for this. Mix with the corn one egg, beaten light, a cup of sweet milk into which has been stirred a bit of soda the size of a pea, two teaspoons of melted butter, a pinch of salt and enough flour to make a thin batter. Beat well together and fry on a griddle as you would cakes for breakfast.

ERBSEN LIEVANZEN (DRIED PEA FRITTERS)

Boil one cup of dried peas, pass through a hair sieve, pour into a bowl, add two ounces of butter rubbed to a cream, add also some soaked bread (soaked in milk), stir all into a smooth paste. Add salt, one teaspoon of sugar, one yolk and one whole egg; one ounce of blanched and pounded almonds. If too thick add more egg, if too thin more bread. Fry a nice brown.

SQUASH FRITTERS

Two cups of boiled squash, half a cup of flour, one teaspoon of baking-powder, one egg and two tablespoons of milk. It is assumed that the squash has been prepared as a vegetable, with seasoning and a little butter, and what is here used is a cold, left over portion of the same. Mix baking-powder with the flour and add to the squash; add milk and stir all together. Beat egg and stir in. Have hot fat in pan and drop fritters from spoon into pan. When browned on both sides remove to hot platter.

FRENCH PUFFS (WINDBEUTEL)

Put one cup of water and one-quarter pound of butter on to boil. When it begins to boil stir in one-quarter pound of sifted flour. Stir until it leaves the kettle clean, take off the fire and stir until milk-warm, then stir in four eggs, one at a time, stirring until all used up. Flavor with the grated peel of a lemon. Put on some rendered butter in a kettle. When the butter is hot, dip a large teaspoon in cold water and cut pieces of dough with it as large as a walnut, and drop into the hot butter. Try one first to see whether the butter is hot enough. Do not crowd—they want plenty of room to raise. Dip the hot butter over them with a spoon, fry a deep yellow and sprinkle powdered sugar over them.

SHAVINGS (KRAUS-GEBACKENES)

Sift about one pint of flour in a bowl, make a depression in the centre; break in five eggs, a pinch of salt, one teaspoon of ground cinnamon and one tablespoon of pulverized sugar. Mix this as you would a noodle dough, though not quite as stiff. Roll out very thin and cut into long strips with a jagging iron. Fry a light yellow. Roll on a round stick as soon as taken up from the fat or butter, sprinkle with sugar and cinnamon or grated peel of a lemon. Mix both thoroughly. Do not let the butter get too brown; if the fire is too strong take off a few minutes.

SNIP NOODLES, FRIED

Sift two cups of flour with three teaspoons of salt in it, make into a dough by adding enough sweet milk to make soft as biscuit dough. Break off small pieces and roll between the hands in the shape of croquettes.

Now put one-half cup of rendered butter in a skillet that has a top to it; when the butter is hot, lay in the pieces of dough (do not put too many in at one time), throw in one-half cup of cold water, put on the cover and let cook until the water is cooked out and noodles are brown on one side. Remove the cover and brown on the other side.

NOODLE PUFFS

Make a noodle dough with as many eggs as desired, roll out somewhat thin, cut in strips four inches long by one inch wide.

Have a skillet half full of boiling hot chicken fat; drop in the strips, a few at a time, baste with the hot grease until brown on both sides. Remove to a platter, sprinkle generously with powdered sugar and cinnamon, and serve.

SNOWBALLS (HESTERLISTE)

Mix one teaspoon of butter, one-fourth teaspoon of salt, one tablespoon of sugar with one egg. Add one tablespoon of cream, one teaspoon of brandy and flour to make stiff dough. Work the whole together with a spoon until the flour is incorporated with the other ingredients and you have a dough easily handled. Break the dough in pieces about the size of a walnut; roll each piece out separately just as thin as possible without tearing (the thinner the better), make three lengthwise slashes in the centre of each piece of dough after rolling out.

Heat a large deep skillet about half full with boiling hot butter or Crisco, drop in the snowballs, not more than three at one time, brown quickly on one side, then on the other, turn carefully with a perforated skimmer as they are easily broken. Remove to a platter, sprinkle with powdered sugar and cinnamon and a few drops of lemon juice.

MACROTES

Blend one pound of good light dough with two eggs, six ounces of butter, and add as much flour as may be needed to make the whole sufficiently dry. Make it into the shape of a French roll, and cut off rather thin slices, which should be placed before the fire to rise, and then fried in oil. Let them drain carefully, and when nearly cold dip each in very thick syrup flavored with essence of lemon.

CAKES

GENERAL DIRECTIONS FOR MAKING CAKES

Use only the best material in making cake.

Gather together all ingredients and utensils that are required. If tins are to be greased, do so the first thing; some cakes require greased or buttered paper, if so, have paper cut the size that is needed and butter the paper.

All measurements are level. See "Measurement of Food Materials".

Use pastry flour. Sift flour twice at least and measure after sifting.

Measure or weigh the sugar, butter, milk and flour. In measuring butter always pack the cup so as to be sure to get the proper quantity. Use the half-pint measuring cup.

If fruit is to be used, wash and dry it the day before it is needed. Dust with flour just before using, and mix with the hand till each piece is powdered so that all will mix evenly with the dough instead of sinking to the bottom.

A few necessary implements for good cake making are a pair of scales, a wooden spoon, two wire egg-whips, one for the yolks and the other for the whites of eggs.

A ten-inch mixing-bowl, and two smaller bowls.

Two spatula or leveling knives.

A set of aluminum spoons of standard sizes.

For convenience, cakes are divided into two classes: Those containing butter or a butter substitute and cake containing no shortening.

The rules for mixing cakes with butter are:

Break the eggs, dropping each in a saucer or cup. If the whites and yolks are to be used separately divide them as you break the eggs and beat both well before using; the yolks until light and the whites to a stiff froth, so stiff that you can turn the dish upside down and the eggs will adhere to the dish.

Rub the butter to a cream which should be done with a wooden spoon in a deep bowl, add the sugar gradually. In winter set the bowl over hot water for a few minutes as the butter will then cream more easily. Add the yolks or the whole eggs, one at a time, to creamed butter and sugar. Sift the baking-powder with the last cup of flour, add flour and milk alternately until both are beaten thoroughly into the mixture, add beaten whites of eggs last to the dough and then set in the oven immediately.

Sponge cakes and cakes that do not contain butter and milk must never be stirred, but the ingredients beaten in, being careful to beat with an upward stroke. Separate the yolks of the eggs from the whites, and beat the yolks with an egg-beater until they are thick and lemon-colored. Then add the sugar, a little at a time, beating constantly. Now beat the whites until they are stiff and dry; add them; the flour should be added last and folded lightly through. Every stroke of the spoon after flour is added tends to toughen the batter. Bake at once. All sponge cakes and torten should be baked in ungreased molds.

TO BAKE CAKES

Make sure the oven is in condition, it can better wait for the cake than the other way around.

Light your gas oven five or ten minutes before needed and reduce heat accordingly when cake is put in oven.

For the coal range, have the oven the right temperature and do not add coal or shake the coals while cake is baking.

If a piece of soft yellow paper burns golden brown in five minutes the oven is moderately hot; if it takes four minutes the oven is hot, if seven minutes is required the oven is fit for slow baking.

Sponge cakes require a slow oven; layer cakes a hot oven, and loaf cakes with butter a moderate oven.

Never look after your cake until it has been in the oven ten minutes.

If cake is put in too cool an oven it will rise too much and be of very coarse texture. If too hot, it browns and crusts over the top before it has sufficiently risen. If, after the cake is put in, it seems to bake too fast, put a brown paper loosely over the top of the pan, and do not open the oven door for five minutes at least; the cake should then be quickly examined and the door carefully shut, or the rush of cold air will cause it to fall. Setting a small dish of hot water in the oven will also prevent the cake from scorching.

When you think your cake is baked, open the oven door carefully so as not to jar, take a straw and run it through the thickest part of the cake, and if the straw comes out perfectly clean and dry your cake is done. When done, take it out and set it where no draft of air will strike it, and in ten minutes turn it out on a flat plate or board.

Do not put it in the cake box until perfectly cold. Scald out the tin cake box each time before putting a fresh cake in it. Make sure it is air-tight. Keep in a cool place, but not in a damp cellar or a refrigerator.

TIME-TABLE FOR BAKING CAKES

Sponge cake, three-quarters of an hour. Pound cake, one hour. Fruit cake, three and four hours, depending upon size. Cookies, from ten to fifteen minutes. Watch carefully. Cup cakes, a full half hour. Layer cakes, twenty minutes.

ONE EGG CAKE

Cream one-fourth cup of butter with one-half cup of sugar, add sugar gradually, and one egg, well-beaten. Mix and sift one and one-half cups of flour and two and one-half teaspoons of baking-powder, add the sifted flour alternately with one-half cup of milk to the first mixture; flavor with vanilla or lemon. Bake thirty minutes in a shallow pan. Spread with chocolate frosting.

LITTLE FRENCH CAKES

Beat one-fourth cup of butter to a cream with one-fourth cup of sugar and add one cup of flour. Stir well and then add one egg which has been beaten into half a pint of milk, a little at a time. Fill buttered saucers with the mixture, bake and when done, place the cakes one on top of another with jam spread between.

GRAFTON CAKE. LAYERS AND SMALL CAKES

Cream four tablespoons of butter with one and one-half cups of sugar, beat in separately two whole eggs, add one cup of milk alternately with two cups of flour in which has been sifted two teaspoons of baking-powder, beat all thoroughly.

This recipe will make two layer-cakes which may be spread with any of the cake fillings or icings.

To make small cakes omit one of the egg-whites, fill well-buttered gem pans a little more than half full, and bake in a moderately hot oven until a delicate brown. The white reserved may be beaten to a stiff froth and then gradually stir in four tablespoons of powdered sugar and the juice of half a lemon. When the cakes are cool, spread with the icing and decorate with raisins, nut meats, one on top of each or sprinkle with candied caraway seeds.

CUP CAKE

Cream one cup of butter with two cups of sugar and add gradually the yolks of four eggs, one at a time. Sift three cups of flour, measure again after sifting, and add two teaspoons of baking-powder in the last sifting. Add alternately the sifted flour and one cup of sweet milk. Add last the beaten whites of the eggs. Flavor to taste. Bake in loaf or jelly-tins.

GOLD CAKE

Take one cup of powdered sugar, one-half cup of butter rubbed to a cream; add yolks of six eggs and stir until very light. Then sift two cups of flour with one and one-half teaspoons of baking-powder sifted in well (sift the flour two or three times). Grate in the peel of a lemon or an orange, add the juice also, and add three-quarters cup of milk alternately with the flour. Bake in moderate oven.

WHITE CAKE

Cream three-quarters cup of butter and one and one-quarter cups of sugar very well. Stop stirring, pour one-half cup of cold water on top of butter mixture and whites of eight eggs slightly beaten on top of water; do not stir, add one teaspoon of vanilla. Sift two and one-half cups of pastry flour, measure, then mix with two heaping teaspoons of baking-powder, and sift three times. Add to cake mixture and then beat hard until very smooth. Turn into ungreased angel cake pan, place in slow oven. Let cake rise to top of pan, then increase heat and bake until firm. Invert pan, when cool cut out.

MARBLE CAKE

Take two cups of sugar, one cup of butter, four eggs (yolks), one cup of milk, three cups of flour, and three teaspoons of baking-powder (scant). Cream the butter and sugar, and add the yolks of eggs. Then add the milk, flour, baking-powder, and the beaten whites of the eggs; flavor with lemon. To make the brown part; take a square of bitter chocolate and melt above steam, and mix with some of the white; flavor the brown with vanilla. Put first a tablespoon of brown batter in the pan, and then the white. Bake in quick oven thirty-five minutes.

LEMON CAKE

Rub to a cream one-half cup of butter with one and one-half cups of pulverized sugar and add gradually the yolks of three eggs, one at a time, and one-half cup of sweet milk. Sift two cups of flour with one teaspoon of baking-powder, add alternately with the milk and the stiffly-beaten whites of three eggs. Add the grated peel of one-half lemon and the juice of one lemon. Bake in moderate oven thirty minutes.

ORANGE CAKE

Beat light the yolks of five eggs with two cups of pulverized sugar, add juice of a large orange and part of the peel grated; one-half a cup of cold water and two cups of flour, sifted three times. Add two teaspoons of baking-powder in last sifting and add last the stiff-beaten whites of three eggs. Bake in layers, and spread the following icing between and on top. Icing: beat the whites of two eggs stiff, add the juice and peel of one orange and sugar enough to stiffen.

POTATO CAKE

Cream two-thirds cup of butter with two cups of granulated sugar; add one-half cup of milk, yolks of four eggs, one cup of hot mashed potatoes, one cup of chocolate, one teaspoon each of cinnamon, cloves, and nutmeg, one teaspoon of vanilla, one cup of chopped walnuts, two cups of flour, two teaspoons of baking-powder, then beaten whites of four eggs. Bake slowly in two pans, and cut in half when cold. Put jam between layers.

POUND CAKE

Rub one pound of butter and one pound of powdered sugar to a cream, add the grated peel of a lemon, a glass of brandy and the yolks of nine eggs, added one at a time, and last one pound and a quarter of sifted flour with one-half teaspoon of baking-powder and the beaten whites of the eggs. Bake slowly.

BAKING-POWDER BUNT KUCHEN

Beat two whole eggs for ten minutes with two cups of sugar, two and one-half tablespoons of melted butter, add one cup of milk, three cups of flour in which have been sifted two teaspoons of baking-powder, flavor with one teaspoon of vanilla; one-fourth cup of small raisins may be added. Bake one hour.

QUICK COFFEE CAKE

Cream one-half cup of butter with one cup of sugar, add three eggs, one and one-half cups of flour, two teaspoons of baking-powder, mixed with the flour, and one-half cup of milk. Mix well together; bake in a long bread or cake pan, and have on top chopped almonds, sugar and cinnamon.

BAKING-POWDER CINNAMON CAKE

Cream three-fourths cup of sugar with a piece of butter the size of an egg, beat together; then add two eggs, one half cup of milk (scant), one and one-half cups of flour, one teaspoon of vanilla and two teaspoons of baking-powder. Put cinnamon, flour, sugar and a few drops of water together and form in little pfaervel with your hand and sprinkle on top of cake; also sprinkle a few chopped nuts on top. Do not bake too quickly. Bake in flat pan.

GERMAN COFFEE CAKE (BAKING-POWDER)

Take three cups of flour sifted, one teaspoon of salt, three tablespoons of sugar, three teaspoons of baking-powder, two eggs, two tablespoons of butter, and two-thirds of a cup of milk. Stir well together, adding more milk if necessary. Keep batter very stiff, sprinkle with melted butter (generously) sugar and cinnamon, and again with melted butter. Put into well-buttered shallow pans and bake about half an hour.

COVERED CHEESE CAKE

Cream one cup of sugar with butter the size of an egg, add two eggs well beaten and one cup of water alternately with two and one-half cups of flour in which has been sifted two teaspoons of baking-powder.

Filling.—Beat two eggs with one-half cup of sugar, add one-half pound of pot cheese, one tablespoon of cornstarch boiled in one cup of milk, cool this and add, flavor with lemon extract.

Put one-half of the batter in cake pan, then the filling and the other half of batter. Bake in slow oven thirty-five minutes. Sift sugar on top when done.

BLITZ KUCHEN

Take one cup of powdered sugar, one-half cup of butter, one cup of pastry flour, one-quarter of a teaspoon of baking-powder, peel and juice of one lemon, five or six eggs. Beat sugar with two whole eggs; add butter, beat until foamy; after that the flour mixed with baking-powder, lemon and four yolks. Last the stiffly-beaten whites of the eggs. Mix this well, bake in form in a moderately hot oven.

KOENIG KUCHEN

Cream one-quarter cup of butter with one cup of sugar, yolks of six eggs, one-quarter pound of raisins, one-quarter pound of currants, juice and peel of one lemon, one spoon of rum, twenty blanched and grated almonds, two cups of flour mixed with one-half teaspoon of baking-powder, two stiffly-beaten whites of eggs. Bake in an ungreased form one to one and one-half hours.

NUT CAKE

Take one-half cup of butter, three eggs, one and one-half cups of sugar, two and one-half cups of flour, two and one-half level teaspoons of baking-powder, and one-half cup of milk. One cup of any kind of nuts. Rub the butter and sugar to a light white cream; add the eggs beaten a little; then the flour sifted with the powder. Mix with the milk and nuts into a rather firm batter. Bake in a paper lined tin in a steady oven thirty-five minutes.

LOAF COCOANUT CAKE

Rub one cup of butter and two cups of sugar to a cream. Add one cup of milk, whites of four eggs, three cups of flour (measure after sifting), and three teaspoons of baking-powder added in last sifting. Add a grated cocoanut and last the stiffly-beaten whites. Bake in a loaf. Line tin with buttered paper.

FRUIT CAKE (WEDDING CAKE)

Take one pound of butter and one pound of sugar rubbed to a cream, yolks of twelve eggs, one tablespoon of cinnamon, one teaspoon of allspice, one-half teaspoon of mace, one-half teaspoon of cloves, one-fourth of a pound of almonds pounded, two pounds of raisins (seeded and chopped), three pounds of currants (carefully cleaned), one pound of citron (shredded very fine), and one-quarter of a pound of orange peel (chopped very fine). Soak all this prepared fruit in one pint of brandy overnight. Add all to the dough and put in the stiffly-beaten whites last. Bake in a very slow oven for several hours, in cake pans lined with buttered paper. When cold wrap in cloths dipped in brandy and put in earthen jars. If baked in gas oven have light very low. Keep oven the same temperature for four or five hours.

APPLE SAUCE CAKE

This apple sauce cake will be found as delicious and tasty as the rich fruit cake, which is so difficult to prepare, and it is very much less expensive.

In a big mixing bowl, beat to a creamy consistency four tablespoons of butter, one egg and one cup of sugar. Add a saltspoon of salt, one teaspoon of allspice, one teaspoon of vanilla and a little grated nutmeg. Beat and stir all these ingredients well together with the other mixture, then add one cup of chopped raisins, after dusting them with flour. Mix these well through the dough and then add one cup of unsweetened apple sauce which has been pressed through a fine wire sieve. After this is well mixed with the other ingredients, stir in one teaspoon of baking-soda dissolved in one tablespoon of boiling water. Last of all, stir in one cup of flour, sifting twice after measuring it. Bake forty-five minutes in moderate oven.

The tendency in making this cake is to get the dough too thin, therefore the apple sauce should be cooked quite thick, and then if the dough is still too thin add more flour. Bake one hour in moderate oven. This cake can be made with chicken schmalz in place of butter. Ice with plain white frosting.

SPICE CAKE

This spice cake is economical, easy to make and delicious, three qualities which must appeal to the housewife.

Cream one cup of brown sugar and one-half cup of butter (or a little less of any butter substitute). Add one-half teaspoon of ground cloves and ground cinnamon, one cup of sour milk; one teaspoon of baking-soda, two cups of flour and one cup of raisins chopped. Have ready a warm oven and bake three-quarters of an hour.

GREEN TREE LAYER CAKE AND ICING

One cup of granulated sugar, one-half cup of butter, three eggs, one cup of milk, two and one-half scant cups of sifted flour, one teaspoon of vanilla extract, two teaspoons of baking-powder. Cream the butter and sugar together as usual, and then break in three eggs and beat until very creamy. Add the flour and milk alternately, reserving a little of the flour to add after the vanilla and baking-powder. Beat well and bake in layer cake tins. The entire success and lightness of this cake depends upon the beating of the sugar, butter and eggs. If these are beaten long enough they will become as creamy and fluffy as whipped cream.

Icing for This Cake.—One and one-half cups of confectioner's sugar (not powdered), butter the size of a large egg, two tablespoons of cocoa, one teaspoon of vanilla, moisten to make the mixture the consistence of very thick cream. Cream or whipped cream may be used for the mixing, but many like this icing when made with lukewarm coffee. The sugar and butter are creamed together thoroughly and then the cocoa and vanilla are added, and lastly the cream or coffee. This is a good imitation of German tree cake. The icing on tree cake is an inch thick, and it is marked to represent the bark of a tree. The way it is served is with a little green candy on it, and it is really very delicious although extremely rich. The thicker or rather firmer this icing is, the better.

EGGLESS, BUTTERLESS, MILKLESS CAKE

One package of seeded raisins, two cups of sugar, two cups of boiling water, one teaspoon of cinnamon, one teaspoon of cloves, two tablespoons of Crisco, chicken schmalz or clarified drippings, one-half teaspoon of salt.

Boil all together five minutes, cool, add one teaspoon of soda dissolved in water, three cups of flour. Bake forty-five minutes, make two cakes in layer pans.

APPLE JELLY CAKE

Rub one cup of butter and two cups of sugar to a cream, add four eggs, whites beaten separately, one cup of milk, two teaspoons of baking-powder and three and one-half cups of flour. Bake in layer tins.

Filling.—Pare and grate three large apples ("Greenings" preferred), the juice and peel of a lemon, one cup of sugar and one well-beaten egg. Put in ingredients together and boil, stirring constantly until thick. Cool and fill in cake.

CREAM LAYER CAKE

Rub one cup of butter and two scant cups of sugar to a cream; the yolks of four eggs beaten in well, add gradually one cup of milk and three cups of sifted flour, and add three teaspoons of baking-powder in last sifting; put whites in last. Bake in layers as for jelly cake. When cold, spread with the following filling: Moisten two tablespoons of cornstarch with enough cold milk to work it into a paste. Scald one-half pint of milk with one-half cup of sugar and a pinch of salt. Beat the yolks of two eggs light; add the cornstarch to this, and as soon as the milk is scalded pour in the mixture gradually, stirring constantly until thick. Drop in one teaspoon of sweet butter, and when this is mixed in, set away until cool. Spread between layers.

COCOANUT LAYER CAKE

Rub to a cream one-half cup of butter and one and one-half cups of pulverized sugar. Add gradually three eggs, one-half cup of milk and two cups of flour, adding two teaspoons of baking-powder in last sifting. Bake in layers.

Filling.—One grated cocoanut and all of its milk, to half of which add the beaten whites of two eggs and one cup of powdered sugar. Lay this between the layers. Mix with the other half of the grated cocoanut five tablespoons of powdered sugar and strew thickly on top of cake, which has been previously iced.

CHOCOLATE LAYER CAKE

Stir one scant half cup of butter to a cream with one cup of sugar. Add alternately one-half cup of sweet milk, yolks of two eggs which you have previously beaten until quite light, add whites of two, and one-half cup of sifted flour. Make a custard of one-half cup of milk, with one cup of grated chocolate, one-half cup of granulated sugar; boil until thick, add the yolk of one egg, then remove from the fire; stir until cool, add this to the cake batter, add one and one-half cups of sifted flour, two teaspoons of baking-powder and one of vanilla flavoring. Bake in layers and ice between and on top with plain white icing flavored to taste. You may substitute almond or colored icing.

CARAMEL LAYER CAKE

Place one-half cup of sugar in pan over fire. Stir until liquid smokes and burns brown. Add one-half cup of boiling water and cook into syrup. Take one cup butter, one and one-half cups of sugar, yolks of two eggs, over one cup of water and two cups of flour. Beat all thoroughly. Add enough of the burnt sugar to flavor, also one teaspoon of vanilla, another half cup of flour, two teaspoons of baking-powder and whites of two eggs. Bake in two layers, using remainder of burnt sugar for icing.

HUCKLEBERRY CAKE

Stir to a cream one cup of butter and two cups of powdered sugar and add gradually the yolks of four eggs. Sift into this three cups of flour, adding two teaspoons of baking-powder in the last sifting and add one cup of sweet milk alternately with the flour to the creamed butter, sugar and yolks. Spice with one teaspoon of cinnamon and add the stiff-beaten whites of the eggs. Lastly, stir in two cups of huckleberries which have been carefully picked over and well dredged with flour. Be careful in stirring in the huckleberries that you do not bruise them. You will find a wooden spoon the best for this purpose, the edges not being so sharp. Bake in a moderately hot oven; try with a straw, if it comes out clean, your cake is baked. This will keep fresh for a long while.

CREAM PUFFS

One cup of hot water, one-half cup of butter; boil together, and while boiling stir in one cup of sifted flour dry; take from the stove and stir to a thin paste, and after this cools add three eggs unbeaten, and stir vigorously for five minutes. Drop in tablespoonfuls on a buttered tin and bake in a quick oven twenty-five minutes, opening the oven door no oftener than is absolutely necessary, and being careful that they do not touch each other in the pan. This amount will make twelve puffs. Cream for puffs: one cup of milk, one cup of sugar, one egg, three tablespoons of flour, vanilla to flavor. Stir the flour in a little of the milk; boil the rest, turn this in and stir until the whole thickens. When both this and the puffs are cool open the puff a little way with a sharp knife and fill them with the cream.

CHOCOLATE ECLAIRS

To make eclairs spread the batter, prepared as in foregoing recipe, in long ovals and when done cover with plain or chocolate frosting, as follows: Boil one cup of brown sugar with one-half cup of molasses, one tablespoon of butter and two tablespoons of flour. Boil for one-half hour, then stir in one-fourth pound of grated chocolate wet in one-fourth cup of sweet milk and boil until it hardens on the spoon. Flavor with vanilla. Spread this upon the eclairs.

DOBOS TORTE

Cream yolks of six eggs with one-half pound of powdered sugar; add three-fourths cup of flour sifted three times; then add beaten whites of six eggs lightly and carefully into the mixture. Butter pie plates on under side and sprinkle with flour lightly over the butter and spread the mixture very thin. This amount makes one cake of twelve layers. Remove layers at once with a spatula.

Filling.—Cream one-half pound of sweet butter and put on ice immediately; take one-half pound of sweet chocolate and break it into a cup of strong liquid coffee; add one-half pound of granulated sugar and let it boil until you can pull it almost like candy; remove from fire and stir the chocolate until it is quite cold. When cold add the chocolate mixture to the creamed butter. This filling is spread thin between the layers, spread the icing thicker on top and sides of the cake. This is very fine, but care must be taken in baking and removing the layers, as layers are as thin as wafers. Bake and make filling a day or two before needed.

SPONGE CAKE

Weigh any number of eggs, take the same weight of sugar and one-half the weight of flour; the grated rind and juice of one lemon to five eggs. For mixing this cake, see the directions given in "To Bake Cakes"; the mixture should be very light and spongy, great care being used not to break down the whipped whites. The oven should be moderate at first, and the heat increased after a time. The cake must not be moved or jarred while baking. The time will be forty to fifty minutes according to size of cake. Use powdered sugar for sponge-cake. Rose-water makes a good flavoring when a change from lemon is wanted.

SMALL SPONGE CAKES

Separate the whites and yolks of four eggs, beat the whites stiff, and beat into them one-half cup of granulated sugar. Beat the yolks to a very stiff froth and beat into them one-half cup of granulated sugar. This last mixture must be beaten for exactly five minutes. Add the juice and grated rind of one small lemon; beat yolks and whites together well, then stir in very gently one scant cup of flour that has been sifted three times. Remember that every stroke of the spoon after the flour is added toughens the cake just that much, so fold the flour in just enough to mix well. If baked in small patty pans they taste just like lady fingers. Bake twenty or twenty-five minutes in moderate oven.

DOMINOES

Make a sponge cake batter, and bake in long tins, not too large. The batter should not exceed the depth of one-fourth of an inch, spread it evenly and bake it in a quick oven (line the tins with buttered paper). As each cake is taken from the oven, turn it upside down on a clean board or paper. Spread with a thin layer of currant or cranberry jelly, and lay the other cake on top of it. With a hot, sharp knife cut into strips like dominoes; push them with the knife about an inch apart, and ice them with ordinary white icing, putting a tablespoonful on each piece, the heat of the cake will soften it, and with little assistance the edges and sides may be smoothly covered. Set the cakes in a warm place, where the frosting will dry. Make a horn of stiff white paper with just a small opening; at the lower end. Put in one spoon of dark chocolate icing and close the horn at the top, and by pressing out the icing from the small opening, draw a line of it across the centre of each cake, and then make dots like those on dominoes. Keep the horn supplied with the icing.

LADY FINGERS

Beat the yolks of three eggs until light and creamy, add one-quarter pound of powdered sugar (sifted) and continue beating; add flavoring to taste, vanilla, lemon juice, grated rind of lemon or orange. To the whites of the three eggs add one-half saltspoon of salt and beat until very stiff. Stir in lightly one-half cup of flour and then fold in the beaten whites very gently. Press the mixture through a pastry tube on a baking-tin, covered with paper in portions one-half inch wide by four inches long, or drop on oblong molds; sift a little powdered sugar on top of each cake, and bake from ten to fifteen minutes in a moderate oven. Do not let brown. Remove immediately from pan, brush the flat surface of one cake with white of egg and press the underside of a second cake upon the first.

JELLY ROLL

Take three eggs creamed with one cup of granulated sugar, one cup of flour sifted with two teaspoons of baking-powder, add one-half cup of boiling water. Bake in broad pan—while hot, remove from pan and lay on cloth wet with cold water. Spread with jelly and roll quickly. Sprinkle with powdered sugar.

ANGEL FOOD

Sift one cup of pastry flour once, then measure and sift three times. Add a pinch of salt to the whites of eight or nine eggs or just one cup of whites, beat about one-half, add one-half teaspoon of cream of tartar, then beat the whites until they will stand of their own weight; add one and one-fourth cups of sugar, then flour, not by stirring but folding over and over until thoroughly mixed in; flavor with one-half teaspoon of vanilla or almond extract. Bake in an ungreased pan, patent tube pan preferred. Place the cake in an oven that will just warm it enough through until the batter has raised to the top of the mold, then increase the heat gradually until the cake is well browned over; if by pressing the top of the cake with the finger it will spring back without leaving the imprint of the finger the cake is done through. Great care should be taken that the oven is not too hot to begin with as the cake will rise too fast and settle or fall in the baking. Bake thirty-five to forty minutes. When done, invert the pan; when cool remove from pan.

SUNSHINE CAKE

Beat yolks of five eggs lightly, add one teaspoon of vanilla, or grated rind of one lemon. In another bowl beat seven whites to a froth with a scant one-half teaspoon of cream of tartar, then beat until whites are very stiff. Gradually add one cup of granulated sugar, sifted three times, to the beaten whites. Fold whites and sugar, when beaten, into the beaten yolks. Sift one cup of flour three times, then put into sifter and shake lightly, fold into the cake. Bake forty minutes in ungreased cake pan. As directed for sponge cake invert pan. Remove cake when it has cooled.

MOCHA TORTS

Beat one cup of powdered sugar with the yolks of four eggs; when very light, add one cup of sifted flour in which has been mixed one teaspoon of baking-powder, add three tablespoons of cold water, one-half teaspoon of vanilla, one tablespoon essence of mocha, add the stiffly-beaten whites and bake fifteen to twenty minutes in two layer pans in a moderate oven. Spread when cold with one-half pint of cream to which has been added one tablespoon of mocha essence, one and one-half tablespoon of powdered sugar and then well whipped. Garnish with pounded almonds.

PEACH SHORTCAKE

Make a sponge cake batter of four eggs, one cup of pulverized sugar, a pinch of salt and one cup of flour. Beat the eggs with the sugar until very light. Beat until the consistency of dough and add the grated peel of a lemon, and last the sifted flour. No baking-powder necessary. Bake in jelly tins. Cut the peaches quite fine and sugar bountifully. Put between layers. Eat with cream.

The same recipe may be used for Strawberry Shortcake.

BREMEN APPLE TORTE

Take seven peeled and cored apples, six tablespoons of sugar, two tablespoons of butter, and cook together until apples are soft. Cream six eggs; add to them one pint of sour cream, one tablespoon of vanilla, one-half teaspoon of cinnamon, and sugar to taste; then pour into the cooked apples and let all boil together till thick. Remove from stove. Take three cups of finely rolled zwieback, and in the bottom of a well-greased pan put a layer of two cups of crumbs, then a layer of the apple mixture, a layer of the remaining crumbs, and lastly lumps of butter over all. Bake one hour.

VIENNA PRATER CAKE

Cream the yolks of six eggs with one cup of granulated sugar. Add three-fourths cup of sifted chocolate, three-fourths cup of flour (sifted twice), one and one-half teaspoon of vanilla. Add the beaten whites. Bake thirty minutes. When cold; cut in half and fill with the following: One cup of milk, yolks of two eggs, one cup of chopped walnuts. Boil, stirring constantly to prevent curdling. Sweeten to taste, and after removing from the fire add one tablespoon of rum. Spread while hot.

SAND TORTE

Cream one-half pound of butter with one-half pound of sugar; drop in, one at a time, the yolks of six eggs. Add one small wine glass of rum, one-fourth pound of corn-starch, and one-fourth pound of flour that have been thoroughly mixed; one teaspoon of baking-powder, the beaten whites of six eggs. Bake one hour in a moderate oven.

ALMOND CAKE OR MANDEL TORTE, No. 1

Take one-half pound of almonds and blanch by pouring boiling water over them, and pound in a mortar or grate on grater (the latter is best). Beat yolks of eight eggs vigorously with one cup of sugar, add one-half lemon, grated peel and juice, one tablespoon of brandy, and four lady-fingers grated, the almonds, and fold in the stiffly-beaten whites of eggs. Bake in moderate oven one hour.

ALMOND CAKE OR MANDEL TORTE, No. 2

Take one-fourth pound of sweet almonds and one-eighth pound of bitter ones mixed. Blanch them the day previous to using and then grate or pound them as fine as powder. Beat until light the yolks of nine eggs with eight tablespoons of granulated sugar. Add the grated peel of one lemon and one-half teaspoon of mace or vanilla. Beat long and steadily. Add the grated almonds and continue the stirring in one direction. Add the juice of the lemon to the stiff-beaten whites. Grate four stale lady fingers, add and bake slowly for one hour at least.

BROD TORTE

Take six eggs, seven tablespoons of granulated sugar, seven tablespoons of bread crumbs, one-eighth pound of chopped almonds, one-half teaspoon of allspice, one tablespoon of jelly, grated rind and juice of one lemon, one teaspoon of cinnamon, one-half teaspoon of cloves, one-half wine glass of brandy. Beat yolks of eggs well and add sugar and beat until it blisters, add bread crumbs, almonds, jelly, spice, lemon, and brandy. Then add beaten whites, and bake slowly about forty minutes.

RYE BREAD TORTE

Beat the yolks of four eggs very light with one cup of sugar; add one cup of sifted dry rye bread crumbs to which one teaspoon of baking-powder and a pinch of salt have been added. Moisten one-half cup of ground almonds with two tablespoons of sherry, add and lastly fold in the beaten whites of eggs. Bake in ungreased form in moderate oven.

ZWIEBACK TORTE

Beat the yolks of six eggs with one and one-eighth cups of sugar, add one-half box of zwieback, which has been rolled very fine, add one teaspoon of baking-powder, season with one tablespoon of rum or sherry wine and one-half teaspoon of bitter almond extract. Lastly fold in the stiffly-beaten whites of the six eggs and bake in ungreased form in moderate oven three-quarters of an hour.

CHOCOLATE BROD TORTE

Separate the yolks and whites of ten eggs. Beat the yolks with two cups of pulverized sugar. When thick add one and three-fourth cups of sifted dry rye bread crumbs, one-half pound of sweet almonds, also some bitter ones, grated or powdered as fine as possible, one-fourth pound of citron shredded fine, one cake of chocolate grated, the grated peel of one lemon, the juice of one orange and one lemon, one tablespoon of cinnamon, one teaspoon of allspice, one-half teaspoon of cloves, and a wine glass of brandy. Bake very slowly in ungreased form. Frost with a chocolate icing, made as follows: Melt a small piece of chocolate. Beat the white of an egg stiff with scant cup of sugar, and stir into the melted chocolate and spread with a knife.

BURNT ALMOND TORTE

Beat up four eggs with one cup of sifted powdered sugar. Beat until it looks like a heavy batter. When you think you cannot possibly beat any longer stir one cup of sifted flour with one-half teaspoon of baking-powder. Stir it into batter gradually and lightly, adding three tablespoons of water. Bake in jelly tins. Filling: Scald one-fourth pound of almonds (by pouring boiling water over them), remove skins, put them on a pie plate and set them in the oven to brown slightly. Meanwhile, melt three tablespoons of white sugar, without adding water, stirring it all the while. Stir up the almonds in this, then remove them from the fire and lay on a platter separately to cool. Make an icing of the whites of three eggs beaten very stiff, with one pound of pulverized sugar, and flavor with rose-water. Spread this upon layers and cover each layer with almonds. When finished frost the whole cake, decorating with almonds.

CHOCOLATE TORTE

Take nine eggs, one-half pound of pulverized sugar, one-half pound of almonds, half cut and grated; one-half pound of finest vanilla chocolate grated, one-half pound of raisins, cut and seeded; seven soda crackers, rolled to a powder; one teaspoon of baking-powder, juice of three lemons and one-fourth glass of wine. Beat whites of eggs to a stiff froth and stir in last. Beat yolks with sugar until very light; then add chocolate, and proceed as with other torten.

DATE TORTE

Beat one-half pound of pulverized sugar with the yolks of six large eggs. Beat long and steadily until a thick batter. Add one-half pound of dates, cut very fine, one teaspoon each of allspice and ground cinnamon, one-fourth pound of chocolate grated, juice and peel of one lemon, three and one-half soda crackers, rolled to a fine powder, one teaspoon of baking-powder, and last the stiff-beaten whites. Bake slowly. Cake can be cut in half and put together with jelly.

GERMAN HAZELNUT TORTE

Beat together for twenty minutes until very light the yolks of eight eggs with one-half pound of granulated sugar, then add the very stiffly-beaten whites of eggs, place the bowl in which it has been stirred over a boiler in which water is boiling on the stove, stir continually but slowly until all the batter is well warmed but not too hot, add a small pinch of salt, and one-half pound of grated hazelnuts, add the nuts gradually, mix well and pour into a greased spring form. Bake very slowly. The grated rind of one-half lemon can be added if desired. Ice with boiled icing.

LINZER TORTE

Cream one pound of butter with one pound of sugar until foamy, then add one by one four whole eggs. Mix well, then stir in three-fourths pound of pounded almonds or walnuts, one teaspoon of cinnamon, one-fourth teaspoon of cloves, one pound of flour, one teaspoon of baking-powder, and a few drops of bitter almond essence. Put in four layer pans and bake in slow oven. Put together with apricot, strawberry, or raspberry jam and pineapple marmalade, each layer having a different preserve. Ice top and sides. If only two layers are desired for home use, half the quantity of ingredients can be used. This is a very fine cake. It is better the second day.

RUSSIAN PUNCH TORTE

Bake three layers of almond tart and flavor it with a wine glass of arrack. When baked, scrape part of the cake out of the thickest layer, not disturbing the rim, and reserve these crumbs to add to the following filling: Boil one-half pound of sugar in one-fourth cup of water until it spins a thread. Add to this syrup a wine glass of rum, and the crumbs, and spread over the layers, piling one on top of the other. Another way to fill this cake is to take some crab-apple jelly or apple marmalade and thin it with a little brandy.

WALNUT TORTE, No. 1

Grate eight ounces of walnuts and eight ounces of blanched almonds. Beat light the yolks of twelve eggs and three-fourths pound of sugar. Add the grated nuts and one-fourth pound of sifted flour, fold in the whites beaten to a stiff froth. Bake in layers and fill with sweetened whipped cream.

WALNUT TORTE, No. 2

Separate the yolks and whites of six eggs, being very careful not to get a particle of the yolks into the whites. Sift one-half pound of granulated sugar into the yolks and beat until thick as batter. Add a pinch of salt to the whites and beat very stiff. Have ready one-fourth pound of grated walnuts, reserve whole pieces for decorating the top of cake. Add the pounded nuts to the beaten yolks, and two tablespoons of grated lady fingers or stale sponge cake. Last add the stiffly-beaten whites of the eggs. Bake in layers and fill with almond or plain icing.

CHESTNUT TORTE

Boil one pound of chestnuts in the shells, peel them while warm, put nuts through potato ricer or colander. Beat well the yolks of six eggs with six tablespoons of sugar, add all the chestnut puree but two or three tablespoons reserved for top of torte, then add three teaspoons of baking-powder and the well-beaten whites of the six eggs; bake in moderate oven fifteen to twenty minutes. Whip one-half pint of cream, add to this the chestnut puree which was reserved, and a little sugar; garnish torte with this mixture. Enough for twelve persons.

NUT HONEY CAKE

Mix two cups of brown sugar, two cups of honey, six egg yolks and beat them thoroughly. Sift together three cups of flour, one-quarter teaspoon of salt, three teaspoons of ground cinnamon, one-half teaspoon each of ground cloves, ground nutmeg and allspice, and one and one-half teaspoons of soda; add one cup of chopped raisins, one-half ounce of citron cut in small pieces, one-half ounce of candied orange peel cut in small pieces, one-half pound of almonds coarsely chopped. Beat the whites of three eggs very stiff and add them last. Pour the dough to the depth of about half an inch into well-buttered tins and bake in a slow oven for one-half hour.

ICINGS AND FILLINGS FOR CAKES

BOILED ICING

One cup of sugar, one-third cup of boiling water, white of one egg beaten stiff. Pour water on sugar until dissolved, heat slowly to boiling point without stirring; boil until syrup will thread when dropped from tip of spoon; as soon as it threads, pour slowly over beaten white, then beat with heavy wire spoon until of proper consistency to spread. Flavor.

WHITE CARAMEL ICING

Put on to boil two cups of brown sugar, one cup of milk and a small lump of butter. Boil until it gets as thick as cream, then beat with a fork or egg whip until thick and creamy. Spread quickly on cake.

MAPLE SUGAR ICING

Boil two cups of maple sugar with one-half cup of boiling water until it threads from the spoon. Pour it upon the beaten whites of two eggs and beat until cold. Spread between layers and on top of cake. Do not make icings on cloudy or rainy days.

UNBOILED ICING

Take the white of one egg and add to it the same quantity of water (measure in an egg shell). Stir into this as much confectioner's sugar to make it of the right consistency to spread upon the cake. Flavor with any flavoring desired. You may color it as you would boiled frosting by adding fruit coloring.

COCOANUT ICING

Mix cocoanut with the unboiled icing. If you desire to spread it between the cakes, scatter more cocoanut over and between the layers.

NUT ICING

Mix any quantity of finely chopped nuts into any quantity of cream icing (unboiled) as in the foregoing recipes. Ice the top of cake with plain icing, and lay the halves of walnuts on top.

ORANGE ICING

Grate the peel of one-half orange, mix with two tablespoons of orange juice and one tablespoon of lemon juice and let stand fifteen minutes. Strain and add to the beaten yolk of one egg. Stir in enough powdered sugar to make it the right consistency to spread upon the cake.

CHOCOLATE GLAZING

Grate two sticks of bitter chocolate, add five tablespoons of powdered sugar and three tablespoons of boiling water. Put on the stove, over moderate fire, stir while boiling until smooth, glossy and thick. Spread at once on cake and set aside to harden.

CHOCOLATE ICING, UNBOILED

Beat the whites of three eggs and one and one-half cups of pulverized sugar, added gradually while beating. Beat until very thick, then add four tablespoons of grated chocolate and two teaspoons of vanilla.

This quantity is sufficient for a very large cake.

INSTANTANEOUS FROSTING

To the white of an unbeaten egg add one and one-fourth cups of pulverized sugar and stir until smooth. Add three drops of rose-water, ten of vanilla, and the juice of half a lemon. It will at once become very white, and will harden in five or six minutes.

PLAIN FROSTING

To one cup of confectioner's sugar add some liquid, either milk or water, to make it the right consistency to spread, flavor with vanilla. Instead of the water or milk, orange juice can be used. A little of the rind must be added. Lemon juice can be substituted in place of vanilla. Chocolate melted over hot water and added to the sugar and water makes a nice chocolate icing; flavor with vanilla.

ALMOND ICING

Take the whites of two eggs and one-half pound of sweet almonds, which should be blanched, dried and grated or pounded to a paste. Beat the whites of the eggs, add half a pound of confectioner's sugar, one tablespoon at a time, until all is used, and then add the almonds and a few drops of rosewater. Spread between or on top of cake. Put on thick, and when nearly dry cover with a plain icing. If the cakes are well dredged with a little flour after baking, and then carefully wiped before the icing is put on, it will not run and can be spread more smoothly. Put the frosting in the centre of the cake, dip a knife in cold water and spread from the centre toward the edge.

MOCHA FROSTING

One cup of pulverized sugar into which sift two dessertspoons of dry cocoa, two tablespoons of strong hot coffee in which is melted a piece of butter the size of a walnut. Beat well and add a little vanilla.

MARSHMALLOW FILLING

Melt one-half pound marshmallows over hot water, cook together one cup of sugar and one-quarter cup of cold water until it threads thoroughly. Beat up the white of an egg and syrup and mix, then add to the melted marshmallows and beat until creamy and cool. Can be used for cake filling or spread between two cookies.

FIG FILLING

One pound of figs chopped fine, one cup of water, one-half cup of sugar; cook all together until soft and smooth.

BANANA FILLING

Mash six bananas, add juice of one lemon and three or more tablespoons of sugar; or add mashed bananas with whipped cream or boiled icing.

CREAM FILLING

Scald two cups of milk. Mix together three-fourths of a cup of sugar, one-third cup of flour and one-eighth teaspoon of salt. Add to three slightly-beaten eggs and pour in scalded milk. Cook twenty minutes over boiling water, stirring constantly until thickened. Cool and flavor. This can be used as a foundation for most fillings, by adding melted chocolate, nuts, fruits, etc.

COFFEE FILLING

Put three cups of warmed-over or freshly made coffee in a small casserole, add two tablespoons of powdered sugar, one-half teaspoon of vanilla. When at boiling point (do not let it boil), add one cup of milk or cream. Then add one tablespoon of cornstarch which has been moistened with cold water. Stir in while cooking till it is smooth and glossy. When the cake is cool, pour mixture over the layers.

LEMON JELLY FOR LAYER CAKE

Take one pound of sugar, yolks of eight eggs with two whole ones, the juice of five large lemons, the grated peel of two, and one-quarter pound of butter. Put the sugar, lemon and butter into saucepan and melt over a gentle fire. When all is dissolved, stir in the eggs which have been beaten, stir rapidly until it is thick as honey, and spread some of this between the layers of cake. Pack the remainder in jelly glasses.

LEMON PEEL

Keep a wide-mouthed bottle of brandy in which to throw lemon peel. Often you will have use for the juice of lemons only. Then it will be economical to put the lemon peel in the bottle to use for flavoring. A teaspoon of this is sufficient for the largest cake.

LEMON EXTRACT

Take the peel of half a dozen lemons and put in alcohol the same as for vanilla.

VANILLA EXTRACT

Take two ounces of vanilla bean and one of tonka. Soak the tonka in warm water until the skin can be rubbed off; then cut or chop in small pieces and put in two wine bottles. Fill with half alcohol, half water; cork, seal, and in a week's time will be ready for use.

PIES AND PASTRY

PUFF PASTE OR BLAETTER TEIG

To make good puff paste one must have all the ingredients cold. Use a marble slab if possible and avoid making the paste on a warm, damp day. It should be made in a cool place as it is necessary to keep the paste cold during the whole time of preparation. This recipe makes two pies or four crusts, and requires one-half pound of butter and one-half teaspoon of salt, one-half pound of flour and one-fourth to one-half cup of ice-water.

Cut off one-third of the butter and put the remaining two-thirds in a bowl of ice-water. Divide this into four equal parts; pat each into a thin sheet and set them away on ice. Mix and sift flour and salt; rub the reserved butter into it and make as stiff as possible with ice-water. Dust the slab with flour; turn the paste upon it; knead for one minute, then stand it on ice for five minutes. Roll the cold paste into a square sheet about one-third of an inch thick; place the cold batter in the centre and fold the paste over it, first from the sides and then the ends, keeping the shape square and folding so that the butter is completely covered and cannot escape through any cracks as it is rolled. Roll out to one-fourth inch thickness, keeping the square shape and folding as before, but without butter. Continue rolling and folding, enclosing a sheet of butter at every alternate folding until all four sheets are used. Then turn the folded side down and roll in one direction into a long narrow strip, keeping the edges as straight as possible. Fold the paste over, making three even layers. Then roll again and fold as before. Repeat the process until the dough has had six turns. Cut into the desired shapes and place on the ice for twenty minutes or longer before putting in the oven.

If during the making the paste sticks to the board or pin, remove it immediately and stand it on the ice until thoroughly chilled. Scrape the board clean; rub with a dry cloth and dust with fresh flour before trying again. Use as little flour as possible in rolling, but use enough to keep the paste dry. Roll with a light, even, long stroke in every direction, but never work the rolling-pin back and forth as that movement toughens the paste and breaks the bubbles of air.

The baking of puff paste is almost as important as the rolling, and the oven must be very hot, with the greatest heat at the bottom, so that the paste will rise before it browns. If the paste should begin to scorch, open the drafts at once and cool the temperature by placing a pan of ice-water in the oven.

FLEISCHIG PIE CRUST

For shortening; use drippings and mix with goose, duck or chicken fat. In the fall and winter, when poultry is plentiful and fat, save all drippings of poultry fat for pie-crust. If you have neither, use rendered beef fat.

Take one-half cup of shortening, one and one-half cups of flour. Sifted pastry flour is best. If you have none at hand take two tablespoons of flour off each cup after sifting; add a pinch of salt. With two knives cut the fat into the sifted flour until the shortening is in pieces as small as peas. Then pour in six or eight tablespoons of cold water; in summer use ice-water; work with the knife until well mixed (never use the hand). Flour a board or marble slab, roll the dough out thin, sprinkle with a little flour and put dabs of soft drippings here and there, fold the dough over and roll out thin again and spread with fat and sprinkle with flour, repeat this and then roll out not too thin and line a pie-plate with this dough. Always cut dough for lower crust a little larger than the upper dough and do not stretch the dough when lining pie-pan or plate.

If fruit is to be used for the filling, brush over top of the dough with white of egg slightly beaten, or sprinkle with one tablespoon of bread crumbs to prevent the dough from becoming soggy.

Put in the filling, brush over the edge of pastry with cold water, lay the second round of paste loosely over the filling; press the edges together lightly, and trim, if needed. Cut several slits in the top crust or prick it with a fork before putting it in place.

Bake from thirty-five to forty-five minutes until crust is a nice brown.

A gas stove is more satisfactory for baking pies than a coal stove as pies require the greatest heat at the bottom.

The recipe given above makes two crusts. Bake pies having a cooked filling in a quick oven and those with an uncooked filling in a moderate oven. Let pies cool upon plates on which they were made because slipping them onto cold plates develops moisture which always destroys the crispness of the lower crust.

TO MAKE AND BAKE A MERINGUE

To beat and bake a meringue have cold, fresh eggs, beat the whites until frothy; add to each white one level tablespoon of powdered sugar. Beat until so stiff that it can be cut with a knife. Spread on the pie and bake with, the oven door open until a rich golden brown. Too much sugar causes a meringue to liquefy; if not baked long enough the same effect is produced.

PIE CRUST (MERBERTEIG)

Rub one cup of butter to a cream, add four cups of sifted flour, a pinch of salt and a tablespoon of brown sugar; work these together until the flour looks like sand, then take the yolk of an egg, a wine-glass of brandy, one-half cup of ice-water and work it into the flour lightly. Do not use the hands; knead with a knife or wooden spoon, knead as little as possible. If the dough is of the right consistency no flour will be required when rolling out the dough. If it is necessary to use flour use as little as possible. Work quickly, handle dough as little as possible and bake in a hot oven. Follow directions given with Fleischig Pie Crust. Fat may be substituted for butter in the above recipe.

PARVE, COOKIE AND PIE DOUGH

Sift into a mixing-bowl one and one-half cups of flour and one-half teaspoon of baking-powder. Make a depression in the centre; into this pour a generous half cup of oil and an exact half cup of very cold (or ice) water; add pinch of salt, mix quickly with a fork, divide in two portions; do not knead, but roll on a well-floured board, spread on pans, fill and bake at once in a quick oven.

No failure is possible if the formula is accurately followed and these things observed; ingredients cold, no kneading or re-rolling; dough must not stand, but the whole process must be completed as rapidly as possible.

Do not pinch or crimp the edge of this or any other pie. To do so makes a hard edge that no one cares to eat. Instead, trim the edges in the usual way, then place the palms of the hand on opposite sides of the pie and raise the dough until the edges stand straight up. This prevents all leakage and the crust is tender to the last morsel.

TARTLETS

Roll puff paste one-eighth of an inch thick; cut it into squares; turn the points together into the middle and press slightly to make them stay. Bake until thoroughly done; place a spoonful of jam in the centre of each; cover the jam with meringue and brown the meringue in a quick oven.

By brushing the top of the paste with beaten egg, diluted with one teaspoon of water, a glazed appearance may be obtained.

BANBURY TARTS

Cut one cup of seeded muscatel raisins and one cup of nuts in small pieces, add one cup of sugar, one well-beaten egg, one tablespoon of water, the juice and grated rind of one lemon. Mix well. Line patty-pans with pie dough, fill with mixture and bake until crust is brown.

FRUIT TARTLETS

If canned fruit is used, take a large can of any kind of fruit, drain all the syrup off and put in a saucepan with an equal quantity of sugar. Cook until it forms a syrup, then pour in the fruit, which has been stoned (if necessary), and cook until the whole is a syrupy mass.

If fresh fruit is used, put on two parts of sugar to one of water and cook until syrupy, then add the fruit, which has been peeled, sliced and stoned, and cook until the whole is a thick, syrupy mass.

Line the patty cases or plain muffin rings with the puff paste. Put a spoonful or two of the fruit in each one and bake a nice brown. Peaches, white cherries, Malaga grapes, huckleberries and apples make nice tartlets.

One large can California fruit fills twelve tartlets.

APPLE FLADEN (HUNGARIAN)

Rub together on a pastry-board one-half pound of sweet butter with one pound (four cups sifted) of flour, add four tablespoons of powdered sugar, a little salt, four egg yolks and moisten with one-half cup of sour cream; cover and set aside in the ice-box for one-half hour. Take two pounds of sour apples, peel, cut fine, mix with one-half cup of light-colored raisins, sugar and cinnamon to taste. Cut the dough in two pieces, roll out one piece and place on greased baking-pan, spread over this four tablespoons of bread crumbs and the chopped sugared apples, roll out the other half of dough, place on top and spread with white of one egg, sprinkle with two tablespoons of powdered almonds. Bake in hot oven.

LINSER TART

Make a dough of one-half pound each of flour, sugar and almonds that are grated with peel on, two eggs, a little allspice, a little citron, pinch of salt. Flavor with brandy. Take a little more than half, roll it out and line a pie-pan, put strawberry jam on and then cut rest of dough in strips and cover the same as you would prune pie. Brush these strips with yolk of egg and bake in moderate oven.

MACAROON TARTS

Line a gem or muffin-pan with rich pie dough; half fill each tart with any desired preserve, and bake in a quick oven. Beat the whites of three eggs to a stiff froth and add one-half pound of powdered sugar and stir about ten minutes or until very light, and gradually one-half pound of grated almonds. Divide this macaroon paste into equal portions. Roll and shape into strips, dusting hands with powdered sugar in place of flour. Place these strips on the baked tarts in parallel rows to cross each other diagonally. Return to oven and bake in a slow oven about fifteen minutes. Let remain in pans until almost cold.

LEMON TART (FLEISCHIG)

Make a rich crust and bake in small spring form. Beat three whole eggs and yolks of three very light with one cup of sugar. Add juice of three lemons and grated rind of one, and juice of one orange. Put whole on stove and stir until it comes to a boil. Put on baked crust, spread a meringue made of the remaining three whites and three tablespoons of sugar on top, and put in oven to brown. May be used as a filling for tartlets.

VIENNA PASTRY FOR KIPFEL

Take one-half pound of pot cheese and one-half pound of butter and two cups of flour sifted four times, add a pinch of salt and work these ingredients into a dough; make thirty small balls of it and put on a platter on the ice overnight. In the morning roll each ball separately into two-inch squares. These squares may be filled with, a teaspoon of jelly put in the centre and the squares folded over like an envelop; or fill them with one-half pound of walnuts, ground; one-half cup of sugar and moisten with a little hot milk. Roll and twist into shape. Brush with beaten egg and bake in a moderately hot oven.

CHEESE STRAWS

One-half cup of flour, two tablespoons of butter, four tablespoons of grated cheese, yolk of one egg, dash of cayenne pepper, enough ice-water to moisten. Mix as little as possible. Roll out about a quarter of an inch thick and cut into long, narrow strips. Shake a little more cheese on top and bake in hot oven. This is also an excellent pie crust for one pie, omitting pepper and cheese.

Serve cheese straws with salads.

LAMPLICH

Make a mince-meat by chopping finely eight medium-sized apples, one-half pound each of raisins, currants and sugar, a little citron peel, two or three cloves and one teaspoon of powdered cinnamon.

Cut some good puff paste into little triangles and fill with the mince, turning the corners of the paste over it so as to make little puffs. Place these closely together and on a buttered baking-dish until it is full. Now mix two tablespoons of melted butter with one teacup of thick syrup flavored with essence of lemon, and pour it over the puffs. Bake until done in a rather slow oven.

MIRLITIOUS

Pound and sift six macaroons; add one tablespoon of grated chocolate and one pint of hot milk. Let stand ten minutes, and then add yolks of three eggs well beaten, one tablespoon of sugar, one teaspoon of vanilla. Line patty-tins with puff paste; fill with the mixture and bake twenty minutes.

APPLE PIE, No. 1

Pare, core and slice four apples. Line a pie-plate with plain pastry. Sprinkle with bread crumbs. Lay in the apples, sprinkle with one-half cup of sugar, flavor with cinnamon, nutmeg or lemon juice or two tablespoons of water if apples are not juicy. Cover with upper crust, slash and prick and bake in moderate oven until the crust is brown and the fruit is soft.

APPLE PIE, No. 2

Put in saucepan one-half cup of sugar and one-fourth cup of water, let it boil a few minutes, then lay in five large apples or six small ones, which have previously been peeled and quartered; cover with a lid and steam until tender but not broken. Line pie-plate with rich milchig pastry, lay on the apples, sprinkle with sugar and cinnamon and bits of butter drop a few drops of syrup over all and bake.

INDIVIDUAL APPLE DUMPLINGS

Butter six muffin rings and set them on a shallow agate pan which has been well buttered. Fill the rings with sliced apples. Make a dough of one and one-half cups of pastry flour sifted several times with one-half teaspoon of salt and three level teaspoons of baking-powder. Chop into the dry ingredients one-fourth of a cup of shortening, gradually add three-fourths of a cup of milk or water. Drop the dough on the apples on the rings. Let bake about twenty minutes. With a spatula remove each dumpling from the ring, place on dish with the crust side down. Serve with cream and sugar, hard sauce or with a fruit sauce.

WHIPPED CREAM PIE

Make a crust as rich as possible and line a deep tin. Bake quickly in a hot oven and spread it with a layer of jelly or jam. Next whip one cup of sweet cream until it is thick. Set the cream in a bowl of ice while whipping. Sweeten slightly and flavor with vanilla, spread this over the pie and put in a cool place until wanted.

GRATED APPLE PIE

Line a pie-plate with a rich puff paste. Pare and grate four or five large tart apples into a bowl into which you have stirred the yolks of two eggs with about half a cup of sugar. Add a few raisins, a few currants, a few pounded almonds, a pinch of ground cinnamon, and the grated peel of a lemon. Have no top crust. Bake in a quick oven. In the meantime, make a meringue of the whites of the eggs by beating them to a very stiff froth and add about three tablespoons of pulverized sugar. Spread this over the pie when baked and set back in the oven until brown. Eat cold.

APPLE CUSTARD PIE

Line your pie-plates with a rich crust. Slice apples thin, half fill your plates and pour over them a custard made of four eggs and two cups of milk, sweetened and seasoned to taste.

CHERRY PIE, No. 1

Line a pie-plate with rich paste, sprinkle cornstarch lightly over the bottom crust and fill with cherries and regulate the quantity of sugar you scatter over them by their sweetness. Bake with an upper crust, secure the edges well by pinching firmly together. Eat cold.

CHERRY PIE, No. 2

Pick the stems out of your cherries and put them in an earthen crock, then set them in the oven until they get hot. Take them out and seed them. Make tarts with or without tops and sugar to your taste. The heating of the fruit gives the flavor of the seed, which is very rich, but the seeding of them while hot is not a delightful job. Made this way they need no water for juice.

SNOWBALLS

Pare and core nice large baking apples, fill the holes with some preserves or jam, roil the apples in sugar and cover with a rich pie crust and bake. When done, cover with a boiled icing and set back in the oven, leaving both doors open to let the icing dry.

BLACKBERRY AND CURRANT PIE

When ready to make the pic, mix as much fruit in a bowl as required, sweeten, stirring the sugar through the berries and currants lightly with a spoon. Dust in a little flour and stir it through the fruit. Cut one of the pieces of pastry in halves, dust the pastry-board with flour and roll the lump of pastry out very thin, cover the pie-plate, a big deep one, with the pastry, trim off the edges with a knife, cutting from you. Fill the dish with the fruit, dust the surface well with flour. Roll out the other piece for the top crust, fold it over the rolling pin, cut a few gashes in it for a steam vent.

Carefully put on the top crust, trim it well about the edge of the pie-plate. Press it closely together with the end of your thumb or with a pastry knife and stand the pie in a moderate oven and bake till the surface is a delicate brown. Then remove the pie and let it stand until it is cool.

The top crust may be made lattice fashion by cutting the pastry in strips, but it will not be as good as between two closed crusts.

CUSTARD PIE

Line the pie-plate with a rich crust. Beat up four eggs light with one-half cup of sugar, a pinch of salt, one pint of milk and grated nutmeg or grated lemon peel, and pour in shell and bake in slow oven.

CREAM PIE

First line a pie-plate with puff paste and bake, and then make a cream of the yolks of four eggs, a little more than a pint of milk, one tablespoon of cornstarch and four tablespoons of sugar, and flavor with two teaspoons of vanilla. Pour on crust and bake; beat up the whites with two tablespoons of powdered sugar and half a teaspoon of cream of tartar. Spread on top of pie and set back in the oven until baked a light brown.

COCOANUT PIE

Line a pie-plate with puff paste and fill with the following custard: Butter size of an egg, creamed with one cup of granulated sugar, one tablespoon of flour, three-fourths cup of grated cocoanut, one tablespoon of milk, vanilla, pinch of salt, and the beaten whites of three eggs.

COCOANUT LEMON PIE

Beat the yolks of six eggs and one cup of sugar until very light, squeeze in the juice of three lemons and the rind of two of them, stir well, then add one-half of a cocoanut grated, and lastly add the whites of six eggs, beaten to a stiff froth. Line a deep pie-plate with rich pastry, sprinkle a little flour over it, pour in the lemon mixture and bake. This makes one pie in deep pie-plate.

LEMON PIE, No. 1

Cover the reverse side of a deep pie-plate with a rich puff paste, and bake a light brown. Remove from the oven until the filling is prepared. Take a large juicy lemon, grate and peel and squeeze out every drop of juice. Now take the lemon and put it into a cup of boiling water to extract every particle of juice. Put the cup of water on to boil with the lemon juice and grated peel, and a cup of sugar; beat up the yolks of four eggs very light and add to this gradually the boiling lemon juice. Return to the kettle and boil. Then wet a teaspoon of cornstarch with a very little cold water, and add also a teaspoon of butter and when the boiling mixture has thickened remove from the fire and let it cool. Beat up the whites of the eggs to a very stiff froth, add half of the froth to the lemon mixture and reserve the other half for the top of the pie. Bake the lemon cream in the baked pie-crust. Add a few tablespoons of powdered sugar and half a teaspoon of cream of tartar to the remaining beaten whites. If you desire to have the meringue extra thick, add the whites of one or more eggs. When the pie is baked take from the oven just long enough to spread the meringue over the top, and set back for two or three minutes, leaving the oven doors open just the least bit, so as not to have it brown too quickly.

LEMON PIE, No. 2

Line a deep pie-plate with nice crust, then prepare a filling as follows: After removing the crust from two slices of bread about two inches thick, pour over it one cup of boiling water; add one dessertspoon of butler, and beat until the bread is well soaked and smooth; then add the juice and rind of one lemon, one cup of sugar, the yolks of two eggs, well beaten, and a little salt; mix well; fill pie with mixture and bake in hot oven until firm. Beat white of two eggs to a stiff froth, add four tablespoons of powdered sugar and spread on top and brown.

MOCK MINCE PIE

Pare, core, and chop fine eight tart apples. Add one cup of seedless raisins, one-half cup of currants, one ounce of chopped citron, one-half teaspoon each of cinnamon, cloves, spice and mace, a tiny bit of salt and grated nutmeg. Pour over whole one tablespoon of brandy, and juice and rind of one lemon. Line bottom and sides of plate with crust, fill in with mixture, and put strips of dough across.

MINCE PIE

Boil two pounds lean, fresh beef. When cold, chop fine. Add one-half pound chopped suet, shredded very fine, and all gristle removed. Mix in a bowl two pounds of seeded raisins, two pounds of currants, one-half pound of citron, chopped very fine. Two tablespoons of cinnamon, two tablespoons of mace, one grated nutmeg, one tablespoon of cloves, allspice, and salt. Mix this with meat and suet. Then take two cups of white wine, two and one-half pounds of brown sugar. Let stand. Chop fine four apples, and add meat to fruits. Then mix wine with whole, stir well, and put up in small stone jars. This will keep all winter in a cool place. Let stand at least two days before using. Line pie-plates with a rich crust, fill with mince meat mixture, put a rich paste crust on top, or strips if preferred, prick slightly and bake. Serve warm, not hot.

PUMPKIN PIE

Press through a sieve one pint of stewed pumpkin, add four eggs and a scant cup of sugar. Beat yolks and sugar together until very thick and add one pint of milk to the beaten eggs. Then add the pressed pumpkin, one-half teaspoon of cinnamon, less than one-half teaspoon of mace and grated nutmeg. Stir the stiffly-beaten whites in last. Bake in a very rich crust without cover.

GRAPE PIE

Squeeze out the pulps and put them in one vessel, the skins into another. Then simmer the pulp a little and press it through a colander to separate the seeds. Then put the skins and pulps together and they are ready for the pies.

HUCKLEBERRY PIE

Line a pie-plate with rich pastry. Pick, clean and wash one pint of huckleberries, drain and lay them thickly on the crust. Sprinkle thickly with sugar, lightly with cinnamon, and drop bits of butter over the top. Bake a nice even brown.

PEACH CREAM TARTS

One cup of butter, and a little salt; cut through just enough flour to thoroughly mix, a cup of ice-water, one whole egg and the yolks of two eggs mixed with a tablespoon of brown sugar. Add to the flour in which you have previously sifted two teaspoons of baking-powder. Handle the dough as little as possible in mixing. Bake in round rings in a hot oven until a light brown. When baked, sift pulverized sugar over the top and fill the hollow centre with a compote of peaches. Heap whipped cream or ice-cream on top of each one, the latter being preferable.

MOCK CHERRY PIE

Cover the bottom of pie-plate with rich crust; reserve enough for upper crust. For filling use two cups of cranberries, cut in halves; one cup of raisins, cut in pieces; two cups of sugar, butter the size of walnut. Dredge with flour, sprinkle with water. Bake thirty minutes in a moderate oven.

PEACH CREAM PIE

Line a pie-plate with a rich crust and bake, then fill with a layer of sweetened grated peaches which have had a few pounded peach kernels added to them. Whip one cup of rich cream, sweeten and flavor and spread over the peaches. Set in ice-chest until wanted.

PEACH PIE, No. 1

Line a pie-plate with a rich pie-crust, cover thickly with peaches that have been pared and sliced fine (canned peaches may be used when others are not to be had), adding; sugar and cover with strips of dough; bake quickly.

PEACH PIE, No. 2

Pare, stone, and slice the peaches. Line a deep pie-plate with a rich paste, sprinkle a little flour over the bottom crust and lay in your fruit, sprinkle sugar liberally over them in proportion to their sweetness. Add a few peach kernels, pounded fine, to each pie and bake with crossbars of paste across the top. If you want it extra fine, with the whites of three eggs to a stiff froth and sweeten with about four tablespoons of pulverized sugar, adding one-fourth of a teaspoon of cream tartar, spread over the pie and return to the oven until the meringue is set. Eat cold.

PINEAPPLE PIE, No. 1

Line your pie-plate with a rich paste, slice pineapples as thin as possible, sprinkle sugar over them abundantly and put flakes of sugar here and there. Cover and bake.

You may make pineapple pies according to any of the plain apple pie recipes.

PINEAPPLE PIE, No. 2

Pare and core the pineapple and cut into small slices and sprinkle abundantly with sugar and set it away in a covered dish to draw enough juice to stew the pineapple in. Bake two shells on perforated pie-plates of a rich pie dough. When the pineapple is stewed soft enough to mash, mash it and set it away to cool. When the crust is baked and cool whip half a pint of sweet cream and mix with the pineapple and fill in the baked shell.

PRUNE AND RAISIN PIE

Use one-half pound of prunes, cooked until soft enough to remove the stones. Mash with a fork and add the juice in which they have been cooked;

one-half cup of raisins, cooked in a little water for a few minutes until soft; add to the prune mixture with one-half cup of sugar; a little ground clove or lemon juice improves the flavor. Bake with two crusts.

PRUNE PIE

Make a rich pie paste. After the paste is rolled out thin and the pie-plate lined with it, put in a layer of prunes that have been stewed the day before, with the addition of several slices of lemon and no sugar.

Split the prunes in halves and remove the pits before laying them on the pie crust.

After the first layer is in sprinkle it well with sugar, then pour over the sugar three or four tablespoons of the prune juice and dust the surface lightly with flour.

Repeat this process till there are three layers, then cut enough of the paste in strips to cover the top of the fruit with a lattice crust and bake the pie in a rather quick oven.

Few pies can excel this in daintiness of flavor.

PLUM PIE

Select large purple plums, about fifteen plums for a good-sized pie; cut them in halves, remove the kernels and dip each half in flour. Line your pie-tin with a rich paste and lay in the plums, close together, and sprinkle thickly with a whole cup of sugar. Lay strips of paste across the top, into bars, also a strip around the rim, and press all around the edge with a pointed knife or fork, which will make a fancy border. Sift powdered sugar on top. Damson pie is made in the same way. Eat cold.

RHUBARB PIE

Make a very rich crust, and over the bottom layer sprinkle a large tablespoon of sugar and a good teaspoon of flour. Fill half-full of rhubarb that has been cut up, scatter in one-fourth cup of strawberries or raspberries, sprinkle with more sugar and flour, and then proceed as before. Over the top dot bits of butter and another dusting of flour. Use a good cup of sugar to a pie. Pinch the crusts together well after wetting them, to prevent the juice, which should be so thick that it does not soak through the lower crust at all, from cooking out.

STRAWBERRY PIE

Make a rich fleischig pie-crust and bake on the reverse side of pie-pan. Pick a quart of berries, wash and drain, then sugar. Take the yolks of four eggs beaten well with one-half cup of sugar and stir the beaten whites gently into this mixture. Pour over strawberries. Put in pie-crust and bake until brown. This mixture with most all fruit pies will be found delicious.

SWEET POTATO PIE

Measure one cup of mashed, boiled sweet potatoes. Thin with one pint of sweet milk. Beat three whole eggs very light with one-half cup of sugar. Mix with sweet potatoes. Season with one-quarter of a nutmeg grated, one teaspoon of cinnamon, and one-half teaspoon of lemon extract. Line pie-plate with crust, fill with mixture, and bake in quick oven.

VINEGAR PIE

Line a pie-plate with a rich crust and fill with the following mixture: One cup of vinegar, two of water and two cups of sugar, boil; add a lump of butter and enough cornstarch to thicken; flavor with lemon essence and put in a shell and bake.

MOHNTORTE

Line a form with a rich puff paste, fill with half a pound of white mohn (poppy seed) which has been previously soaked in milk and then ground. Add a quarter of a pound of sugar and the yolks of six eggs; stir all together in one direction until quite thick. Then stir the beaten whites, to which add two ounces of sifted flour and a quarter of a pound of melted butter. Fill and bake. When done, frost either with vanilla or rose frosting.

RAISIN PIE

Line pie pan with rounds of rich pastry, fill with same mixture as for "Banbury Tarts"; cover with a round of pastry and bake a light brown.

RAISIN AND RHUBARB PIE

Chop one cup of rhubarb and one cup of raisins together, add two tablespoons of melted butter or chicken fat, grated rind and juice of one lemon, one cup of sugar, one well beaten egg, one-quarter cup of bread or cracker crumbs, one-half teaspoon of salt; mix all ingredients thoroughly. Bake between two rounds of pastry. Canned rhubarb may be used.

www.ingramcontent.com/pod-product-compliance
Lightning Source LLC
Chambersburg PA
CBHW081726100526
44591CB00016B/2515